100% NEW

DEVELOPING LITERACY

Customisable teaching resources for literacy

WORD: STRUCTURE AND SPELLING

Ages 10–11

Christine Moorcroft

A & C Black • London

Contents

Spelling strategies

Published 2009 by A & C Black Publishers Limited
36 Soho Square, London W1D 3QY
www.acblack.com

ISBN 978-1-4081-0068-4

Copyright text © Christine Moorcroft 2009
Copyright illustrations © Kevin Hopgood 2009
Copyright cover illustration © Piers Baker 2009
Editor: Jane Klima
Designed by Susan McIntyre

The authors and publishers would like to thank Ray Barker, Collette Drifte and Rifat Siddiqui for their advice in producing this series of books.

A CIP catalogue record for this book is available from the British Library.

Every effort has been made to trace copyright holders and to obtain their permission for use of copyright material. The author and publishers would be pleased to rectify any error or omission in future editions.

Printed and bound in Great Britain by Halstan Printing Group, Amersham, Buckinghamshire.

A & C Black uses paper produced with elemental chlorine-free pulp, harvested from managed sustainable forests.

Introduction

100% New Developing Literacy: Word is a series of seven photocopiable activity books for developing children's ability to read fluently and automatically through using phonic knowledge of grapheme–phoneme correspondences and the skill of blending as their prime approach for decoding unfamiliar words. The series helps children to build up a store of words that they instantly recognise and understand on sight and to segment words into their constituent phonemes. It also helps them to develop skills in spelling words accurately by combining the use of grapheme–phoneme correspondence knowledge as the prime approach, and morphological knowledge and etymological information. They learn a range of useful approaches for learning to read and spell irregular words, including developing an awareness of the roots of words from other languages and older forms of English. There are three books for children aged 4–7 (*Word: Recognition and Spelling*) and four books for children aged 7–11 (*Word: Structure and Spelling*).

100% New Developing Literacy Word: Structure and Spelling Ages 10–11 provides learning activities to support strand 6 (Word structure and spelling) of the literacy objectives of the Primary Framework for Literacy:

Strand 6 Word structure and spelling

- Spell familiar words correctly and employ a range of strategies to spell difficult and unfamiliar words

- Use a range of appropriate strategies to edit, proofread and correct spelling in their own work, on paper and on screen

100% New Developing Literacy Word: Structure and Spelling Ages 10–11 provides support for teaching that develops from previous work based on the National Primary Strategy *Letters and Sounds: Principles and Practice of High Quality Phonics.*

The activities are arranged in three sections – *Revision and consolidation, Spelling rules* and *Spelling strategies.*

The activities

Some of the activities can be carried out with the whole class; some are more suitable for small groups. Most are suitable for either collaborative or individual work, especially useful where the teacher and teaching assistants are working more closely with other groups. Some are generic and can be adapted, using the CD-ROM or masking when copying, for use with different words, graphemes or phonemes; the *Notes on the activities* (see page 5) and, in some cases, the Teachers' notes on the pages provide suggestions and ideas for this and for developing extension activities. Many of the activities can be adapted for use at different levels, to suit the differing levels of attainment of the children (see the Teachers' notes on the pages). Some can be used in different ways as explained in the *Notes on the activities*. The children should be encouraged to use dictionaries to check spellings, meanings and pronunciation and etymological dictionaries to find out about the origins of words and their spellings in order to understand how spellings came about.

Reading

Most children will be able to carry out the activities independently but a few might need help in reading the instructions on the sheets.

Organisation

The activities require very few resources besides pencils, crayons, scissors and dictionaries. Other materials are specified in the Teachers' notes on the pages: for example, interactive whiteboard, etymological dictionaries.

Extension activities

Most of the activity sheets end with a challenge (*Now try this!*) which reinforces and extends the children's learning. These more challenging activities might be appropriate for only a few children; it is not expected that the whole class should complete them, although many more children might benefit from them with appropriate assistance – possibly as a guided or shared activity. On some pages there is space for the children to complete the extension activities, but others will require a notebook or a separate sheet of paper.

Accompanying CD

The enclosed CD-ROM contains all the activity sheets from the book and allows you to edit them for printing or saving. This means that modifications can be made to differentiate the activities further to suit individual children's needs. See page 12 for more details.

Notes on the activities

The notes which follow expand upon those which are provided at the bottom of the activity pages. They give ideas for making the most of the activity sheet, including suggestions for the whole-class introduction, the plenary session or for follow-up work using an adapted version of the activity sheet.

Terms and abbreviations used

Base word
A word which might stand on its own as a meaningful word and to which suffixes and prefixes can be added to form other related words.

Digraph
A two-letter grapheme in which the two letters represent one sound ('two letters – one sound'): for example, **oo** in *boot*, **ch** in *chain* and **ck** in *back*.

Grapheme
A symbol that represents a phoneme. The symbol can consist of one or more letters: for example, **b**, **a**, **ai**, **igh**, **eigh**, **sh**, **tch**. The 26 letters of the English alphabet are combined in various ways to form the graphemes necessary to represent the phonemes of spoken English. For a complete list, see *Letters and Sounds*, pages 25–27.

Morpheme
The smallest morphological unit of language, which cannot be analysed into smaller units.

Morphology
The form (including change, formation and inflection) of words in a language.

Phoneme
The smallest unit of sound in a word that can change its meaning: for example, in the words *lid* and *lad* the difference between the phonemes /**i**/ and /**a**/ creates the difference in meaning between the words. Most linguists agree that spoken English uses about 44 phonemes: for a complete list, see *Letters and Sounds*, pages 23–24.

Phonics
Skills of segmenting and blending sounds within words and an understanding of how to use the phonic 'code' of English in reading and spelling.

Root
The origin of a word: for example, the Middle English, Old English, Latin, Greek or French word it is derived from.

Segment
A meaningful section of a word, which might be a prefix or suffix or another section: for example, **flect** in *deflect*, *reflect*.

To segment
To break down words into their constituent phonemes in order to spell them.

Split digraph
A digraph with a letter that splits (comes between) the two letters in the digraph: for example, in *tide*, the **d** splits the digraph **i-e**, which represents the phoneme /**igh**/.

Trigraph
A three-letter grapheme in which the three letters represent one sound ('three letters – one sound'): for example, **igh** in *right* and **eau** in *bureau*. There are also four-letter graphemes: for example, **eigh** to represent the /**ai**/ phoneme in *neigh*.

The websites listed below may be useful for looking up the etymology of words.

For teachers:
http://www.word2word.com/etyad.html
http://www.etymonline.com/
http://www.verbivore.com/rllink.htm
http://www.westegg.com/etymology/

For children:
http://news.bbc.co.uk/cbbcnews/hi/teachers/literacy_7_11/word newsid_1658000/1658019.stm

Dictionary:
http://www.etymonline.com/index.php?l=c&p=11

Revision and consolidation

The activities in this section help to consolidate the children's learning from previous years about how prefixes and suffixes alter the meaning of a base word and how the spellings of base words change when these affixes are used. The activities build upon this to develop the children's understanding of the ways in which suffixes can form a different class of word (verb/noun/adjective/adverb). There are opportunities to develop strategies for pronouncing unfamiliar words and in knowing when a consonant is doubled.

Oh dear!, **Awesome!** and **Odd one out** (pages 13–15) consolidate the children's knowledge of alternative graphemes for the /oa/ and /or/ phonemes and the **ei** grapheme, respectively, helping them to spell familiar words correctly. It is useful to point out that when they check anything they write they should consider these alternatives in any words they are not sure of. Draw their attention to common patterns and rules: for example, few singular nouns ending with the /**s**/ phoneme end with **os**, **ous**, **ows** or **oas**, all of which are plural endings; adjectives rarely end with **o**, **oa** or **ou**. Also note that **ei** is used for /**ee**/ mainly following **c** (an exception is *seize*). Most of the uses of graphemes on these pages do not follow any rules – they have to be learned through practice – as provided here.

Vowel pairs (page 16) consolidates knowledge of spelling patterns: two adjacent vowels that do not form a digraph but are separate graphemes representing separate phonemes. It develops the ability to spell familiar words correctly. Some of these are easier to recognise than others because the first vowel is part of a prefix: for example, **re-** (*reinstall, reunion, reopen, reinstate*), **de-** (*deodorise*), **extra-** (*extraordinary*). Others are easier because the second vowel in the pair is part of a suffix: for example, -**ish** (*bluish*), -**ing** (*skiing, gluing, echoing*), -**ist** (*oboist*), -**est** (*prettiest*), -**able** (*valuable*), -**ity** (*continuity*), -**ety** (*piety*).

Explosives expert (page 17) helps the children to apply spelling rules and to use proofreading strategies by reading a passage containing words featuring the graphemes **cc**, **x** and **xc** representing the /**ks**/ and /**gz**/ phonemes. It develops their ability to spell familiar words correctly.

American spelling game (page 18) helps the children to learn how to spell familiar words correctly by developing their knowledge of common spelling rules: how US English varies in the spelling of the suffixes -**our** and -**ise**, the -**ce**, -**re** and -**gue** endings, double/single consonants, **ct**/**x** (*connection/connexion*), **ough**/**ow** (*plough/plow*) as well as *pyjamas/pajamas* and *jewellery/jewelry*. However, note *humour/humor* but *humorous* in both standard and US English. Commonly used words that are spelt differently in US English include the following:

Standard English	American English
-our endings	
colour/ful	color/ful
favour/ite	favor/ite/able
harbour	harbor
honour/able	honor/able
humour/humorous	humor/ous
-yse/-ise endings	
analyse	analyze
apologise	apologize
cosy	cozy
criticise	criticize
memorise	memorize
paralyse	paralyze
-ce/-se endings	
defence	defense
offence	offense
practice (noun)	practice (noun)
practise (verb)	practice (verb)
pretence	pretense
-re endings	
centre	center
fibre	fiber
litre	liter
metre	meter
theatre	theater
-gue endings	
analogue	analog
catalogue	catalog
dialogue	dialog
ough	
plough	plow
doughnut	donut
ou	
mould	mold
moustache	mustache
single/double **l**	
fuelled/ing	fueled/ing
enrolment	enrollment
modelled/ing	modeled/ing
signalled/ing	signaled/ing
woollen	woolen
other	
programme	program
pyjamas	pajamas
jewellery	jewelry
storey	story (both tale and floor of building)
grey	gray

Before the children play the game a set of Answers cards should be made. Use the CD-ROM to key in the answers (see below) or write them on a copy of the page. Number the backs of these cards so that the children can spread them face down and turn over the appropriate one to check their answer. Answers cards should read as follows: 1 Standard English, 2 Standard English, 3 Standard English, 4 American English, 5 Standard English, 6 American English, 7 American English, 8 American English, 9 Standard English, 10 American English, 11 American English, 12 Standard English, 13 American English, 14 Standard English, 15 Same in both, 16 American English, 17 Standard English, 18 Standard English, 19 American English, 20 American English, 21 American English, 22 American English, 23 American English, 24 American English, 25 American English, 26 American English, 27 American English, 28 Standard English, 29 American English, 30 American English, 31 Standard English, 32 Standard English.

Getting verbal (page 19) focuses on consolidating the children's knowledge of the use of the verb suffixes -**ate**, -**ify** and -**ise** and the spelling rules these and other vowel suffixes follow, helping them to spell familiar words correctly. During the plenary session it is useful to draw attention to irregular changes such as *pollen/pollinate, clear/clarify, peace/pacify*. Also note that nouns with the same endings can take different suffixes and their endings change in different ways, depending on the meaning of the verb: *decimal/decimalise* (also *decimate*), *person/personify/personalise*.

Name the people (page 20) consolidates and develops the children's knowledge of spelling patterns in order to spell familiar words correctly and helps them to use strategies to approach new and unfamiliar words. They learn to recognise suffixes and develop an understanding of how they modify meaning and spelling. The activity focuses on the suffixes -**er**, -**or**, -**ian** and -**ist** for forming nouns from verbs and other nouns. You could ask the children to write sentences using some of the verbs and then their associated nouns. Display the page on the interactive whiteboard using the CD-ROM to enable the children to try out spellings to see which ones look right.

Singles, **Doubles**, **Double and single** and **Mixed doubles** (pages 21–24) consolidate the children's knowledge of spelling patterns so that they can spell familiar words correctly and use strategies to help them to spell unfamiliar ones. **Singles** focuses on words containing single consonants in each syllable. **Doubles** focuses on words containing double consonants. **Double and single** features words with a pair of consonants in one syllable and a single consonant in another. **Mixed doubles** presents a mixture of single and double consonants. Some of the words in these activities do not follow any spelling rule: they just have to be learnt. Others have the expected spelling patterns: for example, a single consonant following the long **a** in *bacon*, but this does not apply in *habit*, which has a single consonant following a short **a**: similarly in *camera*. Likewise, the children might expect the **m** in *timid* to be doubled after a short /**i**/. They could circle letters they might have expected to be doubled as an aid to memorising unusual examples. In most words with double and single consonants the double consonant ends a stressed syllable: for example, *happen*. However, there are exceptions: *assume*. Answers: (page 21) *timid, limit, habit, dozen, bacon, today, trapeze, elegant, benefit, animal, camera, solitary, pelican, holiday*; (page 22) *gossip, carrot, villain, rubbish, embarrass, mattress, committee, possess, occurring, assess, appalled, address*; (page 23) *opposite, hurricane, cabbage, moccasin, corridor, bulletin, accurate, different, suffocate, curriculum, occasional, attitude*; (page 24) 1 *gazelle*, 2 *molasses*, 3 *tomorrow*, 4 *vanilla*, 5 *parallel*, 6 *colossal*, 7 *necessary*, 8 *harass*. Hidden word: *gorillas*.

Spelling rules

The activities in this section concentrate on knowledge of phonics (phoneme–grapheme correspondences), including less common graphemes, morphology (the formation of words: selecting and adding prefixes or suffixes to base words) and the understanding of how suffixes can convert a word into a word of a different class – noun, verb, adjective, adverb.

Nouns ending -ancy or -ency and **Noun glossary** (pages 25–26) are concerned with spelling patterns and choice of suffixes. They develop the ability to spell familiar words correctly. The children learn to recognise noun suffixes and develop an understanding of how they modify meaning and spelling. This may involve converting adverbs and adjectives to nouns: for example, *frequently/frequency, decent/decency*; it also includes converting nouns for people into abstract nouns with a linked meaning, such as the activity they are involved in, the stage of life they are at or their role in society: for example, *accountant/accountancy, infant/infancy, democrat/democracy*. The choice of -**ancy** or -**ency** is simple when dealing with adjectives or nouns ending in -**ant** or -**ent**.

Verb trios (page 27) develops knowledge of spelling patterns and the ability to spell familiar words correctly. The children decide when the **r** or **l** in the final syllable should be doubled. Some of these follow rules: for example, **r** or **l** followed by **e** is

not doubled (*consoled*) and, in general, **r** or **l** following a vowel digraph is not doubled (*dialled*, *trialled* and *fuelled* are exceptions – note that in *trailed* the **l** does not double). Also discuss what happens to verbs ending in **c** when **-ed** or **-ing** is added – the **c** is not doubled but becomes **ck**: for example, *panicking*. You could display the page on the interactive whiteboard using the CD-ROM to enable the children to try out spellings to see which ones look right.

En- verbs (page 28) develops knowledge of spelling patterns: adding the prefix **en-** to form verbs from nouns and adjectives. It contributes to the children's ability to spell familiar words correctly. They learn that, like most prefixes, **en-** does not change the spelling of the base word but that it can change its meaning and produce a different class of word. The children could use a dictionary to find other verbs beginning **en-** and investigate their roots: for example, *encase*, *enchant*, *encircle*, *endear*, *endow*, *enjoy*, *enrich*, *enshrine*, *ensnare*, *entangle*, *enthral*. Encourage them to use these in sentences that illustrate their meanings. Draw their attention also to words that begin with **en-** where this is not a prefix: for example, *enamel*, *entertain*.

Nationalities (page 29) is concerned with spelling familiar words correctly. It could be linked with work in citizenship (In the media – what's the news?) or geography (What's in the news?, Passport to the world, Connecting ourselves to the world). You could begin by asking the children to read reports of recent international sporting events, from newspapers or the Internet. Ask them to notice the names of countries involved and any words they find for the people from those countries. They could compile a list of nationalities, noting the suffixes.

Material adjectives (page 30) focuses on the suffix **-en** and spelling familiar words correctly. The children could compare this with the prefix **en-** (see page 28) and with their previous learning about verbs formed using this suffix (see *100% New Developing Literacy Word: Recognition and Spelling Ages 6–7*, page 36). They should notice that some words change when this suffix is added to form adjectives. There are too few of these for many rules to be easily spotted but the children should notice that, as with many suffixes, when a vowel suffix is added to a word ending with a consonant, the base word does not usually change. An exception is where the consonant doubles to preserve a short vowel sound preceding it or when **r** or **l** doubles: therefore *wood* becomes *wooden* but *wool* becomes *woollen*. *Brass/brazen* is unusual, with the **ss** changing to **z**. Point out that it can mean 'made of brass' or 'bold' (from the

simile *as bold as brass*).The children could explore more complex formations, including those from verbs, such as *weather-beaten*, *bedridden*, *graven*, *grief-stricken*, *heartbroken*, *heathen*, *misshapen*.

Adjective suffixes (page 31) helps the children to extend their knowledge of suffixes and their meanings. During the plenary session, invite feedback about the relationships between suffixes and meanings: for example, **-ish** added to a noun to form an adjective is usually comparative (*childish* = like a child, *fiendish* = like a fiend); **-ish** added to a number means 'about' (*fortyish* = about forty, *thirtyish* = about thirty); **-ish** added to an adjective usually indicates degree (*greyish*, *plumpish*, *whitish*). Also discuss how the base words changed and how this compares with the use of other vowel suffixes: base words ending in adjacent consonants or a vowel digraph followed by a consonant are unchanged (*fiendish*, *youngish*, *oldish*, *foolish*, *ghoulish*, *sheepish*); those ending with a long vowel phoneme ending with a consonant are unchanged (*slowish*, *greyish*); a single consonant might be doubled to preserve the short vowel phoneme preceding it (*snobbish*, *piggish*); the final **e** is dropped (*white/whitish*, *blue/bluish*, *slave/slavish*, *style/stylish*); **-some**, like most suffixes beginning with a consonant, does not affect the spelling of the base word.

Spelling poem, **Spelling rhymes** and **Spell that rhyme** (pages 32–34) present humorous poems that highlight alternative phonemes represented by graphemes and alternative graphemes for phonemes: **-ough**, **-ear**, **ea**, **o(th)**, **oe**, **o-e**, **s**, **or**, **ar**, **oo/ew/u/ue**, **eas/ease**, **in/ine**, **ought/aught**, **air/ere/ear**, **ough/ow**, **oa/oo**, **e/ie** and **o** at the end of a short word. In their own verses the children could use the following graphemes: **eigh** (*height*, *sleigh*, *weight*), **ei** (*ceiling*, *deceive*, *leisure*, *receive*, *rein*, *skein*), **c** (*discount*, *viscount*), **o(m)** (*come*, *dome*, *home*, *homing*, *some*, *woman*, *women*), **o(mb)** (*bomb*, *comb*, *rhomb*, *tomb*, *womb*), **ie** (*fiend*, *friend*), **oe** (*canoe*, *doe*, *hoe*, *shoe*, *sloe*, *toe*, *woe*).

Read the runes and **Greek spellings** (pages 35–36) help the children to learn spelling rules to spell familiar words correctly and to use strategies for spelling unfamiliar words. The activity consolidates their previous learning of alternative graphemes for the different phonemes and draws on the growing vocabulary of words they can read on sight. The runes and Greek letters are not the exact equivalents of letters of the alphabet used in English but represent phonemes. Both of these activities draw on the children's previous learning in history (Why have people invaded and settled in Britain in the past? A Viking case study) and could be linked with current work in history (Who were the

Ancient Greeks?). Answers: (page 35) *bread, sun, wolf, wealth, while, fierce, throng, happy, seize* (or *seas* or *sees*), *peasant, bright, thanks, fighting, bring, east, west, fox, ring*; (page 36) *myth, atom, monk, scholar, panto, photo, phone, script, atlas, critic, crypt, plastic, thermal, acrobat, microbe, kilo, telescope, astronaut, epidemic, symbol, syllable.*

Spell that sign (page 37) helps the children to learn spelling rules to help them to spell familiar words correctly. The activity consolidates their previous learning of alternative graphemes for the different phonemes and draws on the growing vocabulary of words they can read on sight.

Spellchecker poem (page 38) helps the children to learn spelling rules in order to spell familiar words correctly. It consolidates their previous learning of alternative graphemes for different phonemes and draws on the growing vocabulary of words they can read on sight. They should use their knowledge of other words with similar meanings to help them and should draw on their knowledge of past tense suffixes, comparative adjective suffixes and irregular past tenses. They learn to

recognise, and distinguish between, homophones and learn that they cannot rely on a spellchecker to do this. To demonstrate this, use the CD-ROM to display the poem on an interactive whiteboard or computer and let the children run the spellchecker.

Compound words (page 39) helps the children to learn spelling rules and to spell familiar words correctly by splitting compound words into their separate words and provides an opportunity for editing and proofreading on screen. They also learn the purpose of hyphens in combining words. The children could use the spellchecker on a computer to check other word combinations to find out if they can be combined to make a single word and, if so, whether it needs a hyphen. Encourage them to check their results in a dictionary and to discuss any discrepancies between the spellchecker and the dictionary – and between dictionaries (including the online dictionary Wiktionary).

Spelling strategies

In this section there are activities that develop the children's knowledge about the roots of words and how words are constructed from meaningful segments, including prefixes and suffixes. There are activities to develop a range of strategies to help them to read and spell unfamiliar or difficult words using analogy and mnemonics and 'spellspeak' to remember unstressed vowels and unpronounced letters. It is important to acknowledge that everyone can experience difficulty in spelling some words and that those who make the fewest mistakes usually do so because they use a range of strategies to help them to read and spell new words – always using what they have learned from other words.

Word families from RE and **Word families from science** (pages 40–41) help the children to spell familiar words correctly and to use strategies that help them to spell unfamiliar words through using prefixes and suffixes to alter the meanings and spellings of words. Using the words in sentences helps the children to identify the class of word they have formed and to understand how these work in sentences. Possible answers: (page 40) *baptised, baptises, baptising, baptism, baptismal, Baptist, baptistery; worshipful, worshipped, worshipper, worshipping, worships; faithful, faithfully, faithfulness, faithless, faithlessness; symbolic, symbolically, symbolise, symbolised, symbolising; prayed, prayer, prayers, praying, prays; christening, Christian, Christianity, Christmas; Jewish, Jewry, Judaic, Judaism; festival, festivals, festivity, festivities*; (page 41) *magnetic, magnetically, magnetise, magnetism; gravitate, gravitated, gravitates, gravitating, gravitation, gravitational; leverage, levered, levering, levers; electrical, electrically, electricity, electrics, electronic, electronically; pollinate, pollinated, pollinates, pollinating; fertilisation, fertilise, fertilised, fertiliser, fertilising, fertility; absorbed, absorbent, absorbing, absorbs, absorption; audiovisual, television, visual, visually.*

Basic and **Back to basics** (pages 42–43) help the children to spell familiar words correctly through using prefixes and suffixes to alter the meanings and spellings of words. Using the words in sentences (page 42) helps the children to identify the class of word they have formed, to understand how these classes work in sentences and to demonstrate the different meanings of different words of the same class formed from the same base word: for example, *actor/action/activity; act/activate; belief/believer; collector/collection; examiner/examination; parting/partition.*

Peculiar plurals (page 44) is about spelling patterns and spelling familiar words correctly. The children learn to recognise and spell unusual plural endings in words of Latin and Greek origin: **-a** (for example, *bacteria, data, gymnasia*); **-ae** (*algae, antennae, larvae*); **-es** (*bases, crises, metamorphoses*); **-i** (*cacti, radii, termini*).

Be a word archaeologist (page 45) is about irregular spellings and develops the children's knowledge of unstressed vowels and consonants and their understanding of the derivation of words. This helps to develop their ability to spell familiar words correctly and to approach unfamiliar ones with confidence as the derivation of a word often reveals how its unusual spelling came about. The answers to the questions can act as mnemonics – for example, for the ending of *dande<u>li</u>on*, the **ew** grapheme in *steward*, the **r** in *February*, the **b** in *comb* and **eau** in *bureau*.

Homophone sources: 1 and **2** (pages 46–47) develop knowledge of the reasons for spelling patterns, as the children discover the different derivations of homophones, thus developing their ability to spell familiar words correctly. You could challenge them to explore the derivations of other homophones to find out if this influences their spellings. They could build up an electronic database of homophone roots, using a table in Word.

Viking invasion, **Arabic wordsearch** and **Indian inspiration** (pages 48–50) develop the children's ability to spell familiar words correctly through exploring etymology. Explain that *loan words* are words that are taken from another language. These words have come into English through the Vikings who invaded and settled in northern Britain in the ninth century and through Britain's commercial, military and migratory links with Arabic-speaking countries and with India. The activities could be linked with work in geography (Passport to the world, Connecting ourselves to the world and What's in the news?) and citizenship (The media – what's the news?). Encourage the children to investigate the original meanings of the words. Tell them that Arabic has its own alphabet and that Arabic words written using the English alphabet may not always be spelt in the same way. You could challenge them to look for other words whose spelling patterns suggest that they might come from Old Norse, Arabic or Indian languages and to check these using a detailed dictionary or an etymological dictionary. Answers: (page 48) *breadth/breidd, brother/broðir, church/kirkja, comb/kambr, freckles/frecknur, knock/knoka, law/lagu, reindeer/hreindyri, outlaw/utlagi, weight/vett, vætt*; (page 49) 1 *alcohol/al-kuhl*, 2 *algebra/al-jabr*, 3 *alcove/al-kubba*, 4 *amber/anbar*, 5 *apricot/albarkuk*, 6 *coffee/kahwa*, 7 *genie/jinn*, 8 *kebab/kaba*, 9 *mattress/matrah*, 10 *zero/cipher*, 11 *safari/safar*, 12 *sequin/sikka*, 13 *sherbet/sarab*, 14 *sofa/suffa*, 15 *sugar/sukkar*, 16 *talc/talk*.

A Latin root: 1 and **2**, **A Greek puzzle** and **Named for the gods** (pages 51–54) develop the children's ability to spell familiar words correctly and to employ a range of strategies to spell difficult and unfamiliar words through exploring etymology. They also increase their knowledge of prefixes. You could challenge them to look for other words whose spelling patterns suggest that they might come from Latin or Greek and to check these using a detailed dictionary or an etymological dictionary (see also **Peculiar plurals**, page 44). Answers: (page 51) 1 *suspend*, 2 *appendix*, 3 *suspense*, 4 *depend*, 5 *compendium*, 6 *pendant*, 7 *expensive*, 8 *appendicitis*, 9 *pendulum*, 10 *dispensary*, 11 *impending*; (page 52 – clockwise from *fact*) *factory, artefact, effect, benefactor, infect, confectionery, manufacture, perfect, affect, defect*; (page 53) °*monolith, megalith, psychology, psychiatrist, monologue, monochrome, microphone, megaphone, biology, hydrometer, hydraulic, microbe, micrometer, geology, geography, dehydrated*; (page 54) *atlas, cereal, echo, fortune, hypnotise, jovial, chronology, music, mnemonic, martial, mortuary, volcano*.

Word groups (page 55) develops the children's range of strategies for spelling new or unfamiliar words by focusing on grouping and classifying words by their meanings. These pages could be edited using the CD-ROM to provide other useful word groups: *class/classic/classical/classify, herb/herbage/herbal/herbicide, adverb/verb/verbal, crypt/cryptic/cryptogram/encrypt, insular/insulate/insulation/insulator, fume/fumed/fumigate/perfume, revitalise/vital/vitalise/vitality*.

Vanishing vowels (page 56) develops the children's ability to spell familiar words and their strategies for approaching new and unfamiliar words through using 'spellspeak' to learn words containing unstressed vowels. It encourages them to focus on, and therefore remember, the unstressed vowel. An example of 'spellspeak' is given by *climATE* on the activity sheet. You should be aware of possible regional variations in pronunciation.

Strange spellings (page 57) helps the children to develop a strategy for reading and spelling difficult words through identifying and describing their noticeable features. After they have completed the activity you could read out the words for them to try to spell (provide a copy of the page, edited using the CD-ROM, with the words deleted from the word-bank).

Help words (page 58) helps the children to spell familiar words accurately and to develop a strategy for approaching new and unfamiliar words through using their knowledge of morphology and etymology. The focus is on unstressed vowels – each 'help word' contains the tricky grapheme that is unstressed or unpronounced in the 'difficult' word, but in the help word it is pronounced: for example, the **or** is pronounced in *ignore*; this helps the children to spell the word *ignorance* where the **or** is unstressed.

Help sentences: 1 and **2** (pages 59–60) develop the children's range of strategies for approaching new and unfamiliar words as well as for spelling familiar words correctly through the use of mnemonics. They focus on words containing unstressed vowels and unpronounced consonants. Possible words to use in help sentences: *sand/sandwich*, *secret/secretary*, *peas/peasants*, *lice/accomplice*, *age/passage*, *face/surface*, *pal/principal*, *mice/pumice*, *fall/fallacy*, *gent/agent*, *lace/palace*, *heath/heather*, *pest/tapestry*, *cat/caricature*, *chest/orchestra*, *table/vegetables*, *temper/temperamental*, *vile/privilege*. Explain that the help words do not necessarily come from the same root as the difficult word: for example, *sandwich* comes from the Earl of Sandwich, a keen gambler, who had his meals brought to him wrapped in bread in order to eat without leaving the gaming table. Encourage the children to make up their own 'help sentences' for words they find difficult, especially those containing unstressed vowels or consonants that are unpronounced, and to share these during plenary sessions.

Difficult words (page 61) encourages the children to use their knowledge of morphology and etymology to spell new and unfamiliar words. You could ask them to research a word and to prepare a short presentation to the class to explain how its irregular spelling came about, including the language it came from. Encourage them to use the interactive whiteboard to aid their presentation, which could include drawings, photographs and sound. You could adapt the table to focus on words with which your class will be unfamiliar.

Robot words (page 62) develops the children's range of strategies for reading and spelling new and unfamiliar words: grouping and classifying words according to spelling patterns and using analogy to help them to read and spell them. You could use the CD-ROM to edit the page to help the children to read and spell topical words or words they are going to come across in a shared text.

Acrostics (page 63) develops the children's range of strategies for reading and spelling new and unfamiliar words through using mnemonics to learn tricky words containing less common phoneme–grapheme correspondences. They could edit this page, using the CD-ROM, to write acrostics for words they come across in their reading or in other subjects and which they find difficult.

Flashes of inspiration (page 64) encourages the children to develop and share personal strategies for learning new and irregular words. They could also make a display of 'flashes of inspiration' in which they draw and cut out larger 'flashes' to fix onto a display board, to show how they remember the spellings of words they have trouble with.

Using the CD-ROM

The CD-ROM included with this book contains an easy-to-use software program that allows you to print out pages from the book, to view them (e.g. on an interactive whiteboard) or to customise the activities to suit the needs of your pupils.

Getting started

It's easy to run the software. Simply insert the CD-ROM into your CD drive and the disk should autorun and launch the interface in your web browser.

If the disk does not autorun, open 'My Computer' and select the CD drive, then open the file 'start.html'.

Please note: this CD-ROM is designed for use on a PC. It will also run on most Apple Macintosh computers in Safari however, due to the differences between Mac and PC fonts, you may experience some unavoidable variations in the typography and page layouts of the activity sheets.

The Menu screen

Four options are available to you from the main menu screen.

The first option takes you to the Activity Sheets screen, where you can choose an activity sheet to edit or print out using Microsoft Word.

(If you do not have the Microsoft Office suite, you might like to consider using OpenOffice instead. This is a multi-platform and multi-lingual office suite, and an 'open-source' project. It is compatible with all other major office suites, and the product is free to download, use and distribute. The homepage for OpenOffice on the Internet is: www.openoffice.org.)

The second option on the main menu screen opens a PDF file of the entire book using Adobe Reader (see below). This format is ideal for printing out copies of the activity sheets or for displaying them, for example on an interactive whiteboard.

The third option allows you to choose a page to edit from a text-only list of the activity sheets, as an alternative to the graphical interface on the Activity Sheets screen.

Adobe Reader is free to download and to use. If it is not already installed on your computer, the fourth link takes you to the download page on the Adobe website.

You can also navigate directly to any of the three screens at any time by using the tabs at the top.

The Activity Sheets screen

This screen shows thumbnails of all the activity sheets in the book. Rolling the mouse over a thumbnail highlights the page number and also brings up a preview image of the page.

Click on the thumbnail to open a version of the page in Microsoft Word (or an equivalent software program, see above.) The full range of editing tools are available to you here to customise the page to suit the needs of your particular pupils. You can print out copies of the page or save a copy of your edited version onto your computer.

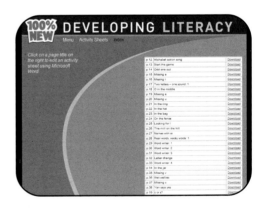

The Index screen

This is a text-only version of the Activity Sheets screen described above. Choose an activity sheet and click on the 'download' link to open a version of the page in Microsoft Word to edit or print out.

Technical support

If you have any questions regarding the *100% New Developing Literacy* or *Developing Mathematics* software, please email us at the address below. We will get back to you as quickly as possible.

educationalsales@acblack.com

Oh dear!

The answers to the puzzle all contain the phoneme $\boxed{oa}$.
- **Choose the correct spelling for this phoneme.**
- **Write the numbers and the words in the shapes.**

Check your answers in a dictionary.

1 Big brownish-black insect (cockr_____ch)
2 Your arms are joined to these (sh_____lders)
3 Large animal with hooves (buffal_____)
4 Opening in the ground (h_____)
5 Found on food that has gone bad (m_____ld)
6 Not deep (shall_____)
7 Showing off (b_____sting)
8 Snapshot (ph_____tograph)

9 Room where coats are left (cl_____kroom)
10 Shedding hair (as dogs do) (m_____lting)
11 Tooth used for grinding food (m_____lar)
12 Swimming backwards (backstr_____)
13 Type of sugar (gluc_____)
14 Sad (sorr_____ful)
15 Fear (ph_____bia)
16 Possession (_____nership)

poultry

wheelbarrow

casserole

radio

toaster

NOW TRY THIS!
- **Write other words on any spare lines in the shapes.**

Each word must have at least six letters.

Teachers' note Start by asking the children for words that contain the /oa/ phoneme. They could come out and write up the words. Ask about the different graphemes that can be used for this phoneme. Make sure they remember o-e (as in *mole*). Display these and go round the class, pointing to a grapheme and asking a child for a word that contains it, representing /oa/.

100% New Developing Literacy
Word: Structure and Spelling
Ages 10–11
© A & C BLACK

13

Awesome!

Each sentence has words with gaps. Throughout each sentence, the | or | phoneme is spelt in the same way.

Check your answers in a dictionary.

• **Fill in the gaps.**

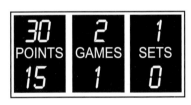

What good f____tune! It was gl____ious weather on this imp____tant day for sp____t: it was a sc____cher.

Mum ate str____berries on the l____n while I spr____led nearby and scr____led a postcard to Dad.

We watched f____ games of the t____nament on Centre C____t and hoped there wouldn't be a downp____.

After that f____hand shot I could f____cast the sc____ bef____ the end of the game.

The shot was p____, but it fl____ed the player nearest the d____.

Mum w____ned, "He has only a qu____ter of an hour of daylight to win the aw____d and not be thw____ted again."

NOW TRY THIS!

• **Write six words containing the | or | phoneme spelt | au |.**

No easy words allowed! They must have at least six letters.

Teachers' note Introduce the activity by asking the children for words that contain the /or/ phoneme. They could come out and write or type the words. Ask them about the different graphemes that can be used for this phoneme. Point out that different sentences on this page contain /or/ spelt in different ways.

100% New Developing Literacy
Word: Structure and Spelling
Ages 10–11
© A & C BLACK

Odd one out

- **Look at each set of words.**
- **What similarity can you see?**
- **Read each set of words aloud. Circle the odd one out.**
- **Write what makes it different from the others.**

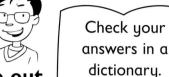

Look for a pair of vowels.

Check your answers in a dictionary.

receipt   protein   sleigh

either   ceiling   eiderdown

rottweiler   freight   neighbour

_____

_____

_____

weight   conceited   surveillance

beige   neigh   receive

deceive   kaleidoscope   Sheila

_____

_____

_____

height   reindeer   feign

eighteen   foreign   vein

sheikh   reign   seize

_____

_____

_____

NOW TRY THIS!

- **Read these words aloud, then write them in pairs, according to the phonemes you hear.**

    caffeine   counterfeit   leisure   deign
    forfeit   veil   heifer   perceive

Teachers' note Introduce the activity by displaying some words that contain the **ei** grapheme: *rein, receive, weigh, neither, eight, vein*. Ask them about the different phonemes it can represent. They should read each set of words on this page aloud; listen to check their pronunciation. Also show them how to use dictionary pronunciation guides.

100% New Developing Literacy
Word: Structure and Spelling
Ages 10–11
© A & C BLACK

Vowel pairs

- **Read each word or name aloud.**
- **Draw a line to split each word into its separate syllables.**
- **What do you notice about where each word is split? What happens to the vowels?** _____

Use a dictionary to check how to pronounce the words.

blu|ish	albeit	boa	reinstall	deity
rodeo	mutual	piety	valuable	mosaic
deodorise	echoing	fluid	ruined	prettiest
February	extraordinary	geology	realise	casual
continuity	gluing	oboist	zoologist	dais
reunion	naive	quiet	millennium	stereo
nuclear	genuine	reinstate	skiing	reopen

NOW TRY THIS!

- **Look up these words in a dictionary and an etymological dictionary.**

  echoing   coordinate   readjust   valuing

- **Explain why the two vowels are split.**

Teachers' note Remind the children about pairs of vowels that represent two different sounds (see *100% New Developing Literacy Word: Structure and Spelling Ages 9–10*, page 27). Use that activity to show that in many vowel pairs that are pronounced separately one of the vowels is part of a prefix or suffix (for example, *doing, stoic*); but note that some are not: *chaos, koala, bias*.

100% New Developing Literacy
**Word: Structure and Spelling
Ages 10–11**
© A & C BLACK

Explosives expert

- **The words with gaps contain the** `ks` **or** `gz` **phoneme.**
- **Write** `x` , `xc` **or** `cc` **in the gaps.**

Check your answers in a dictionary.

The e__iting story of Ma__ the Fi__er

Ma__ was rela__ing after his daily e__ercise, e__amining the football fi__ture list for his favourite team – Halifa__ Town. He had never missed a match e__ept when he had chickenpo__.

His phone rang: "Ma__ !The E__entrics are going to e__ecute the Queen at the Ideal Palace E__hibition in e__actly one hour. Our informer e__pects that they have access to the Lu__ury Palace café and will e__plode a to__ic mi__ture. They must not su__eed. Come and help! We'll send a ta__i."

He jumped into the ta__i . "Faster!" he e__laimed. "E__press! To the E__hibition Centre in Fo__glove Lane. Step on the a__elerator."

"I'm doing e__actly 40 miles per hour. That's the limit. I can't make e__eptions. I don't want an a__ident or a fine for e__ess speed."

Max felt as if he would e__pire. He couldn't a__ept what the driver said. "I'm Ma__ the Fi__er. I'm an e__pert on poisons and e__plosives. I am e__pected to save the Queen. It's a comple__ plot. I have to be quick."

The driver became e__ited. "This is e__eptional! It's e__actly what I've always wanted. I know a quick way in through the e__it."

As they drove in, Ma__ e__tended his inde__ finger to its ma__imum length (si__ metres).

"That's him – e__actly where I e__pected. I've fi__ed him to the spot. Now I can e__amine his bag and e__tract the deadly mi__ture. That's a su__essful hour's work. Thank you for your e__ellent help."

NOW TRY THIS!

- **Correct the spellings of the following words, then use them in sentences.**

  excist   exerpt   exsample   axent   axess   vaxination

Teachers' note To prepare for this activity, the children could do some homework in which they collect examples of words with the /ks/ and /gz/ phonemes; these could have different spellings, but will mostly involve the **x** grapheme. Remind them to think about the sound rather than the look of the word, however, otherwise they might look only for words featuring **x**.

100% New Developing Literacy
Word: Structure and Spelling
Ages 10–11
© A & C BLACK

17

American spelling game

1 colourful	**2** offence	**3** analyse	**4** honorable
5 memorise	**6** pajamas	**7** analog	**8** modeled
9 tyre	**10** traveling	**11** jewelry	**12** equally
13 plow	**14** moustache	**15** humorous	**16** liter
17 fibre	**18** metre	**19** pretense	**20** harbor
21 connexion	**22** theater	**23** paralyzed	**24** cozy
25 donut	**26** mold	**27** center	**28** favourite
29 sulfur	**30** color	**31** storey	**32** grey

18

Teachers' note Play this in groups of four. Spread the cards out face down. The children take turns to pick up a card. They read the word and say whether it has the Standard English or American English spelling. They check their answer against the same numbered card in the Answers set. If they were right, they keep the card. The winner has the most cards at the end.

**100% New Developing Literacy
Word: Structure and Spelling
Ages 10–11
© A & C BLACK**

Getting verbal

• **Add the suffix** ate , ify **or** ise **to make each noun or adjective into a verb.**

> You might have to change the spellings of the base words.

active	→		modern	→	

beauty	→		humid	→	

nominal	→		pollen	→	

decimal	→		stagnant	→	

person	→		immune	→	

civil	→		unit	→	

solid	→		intense	→	

peace	→		colony	→	

tolerant	→		clear	→	

NOW TRY THIS!

• **Do some research to find out which of the verb suffixes on this page is the most common.**

Teachers' note Remind the children of the roles of nouns, verbs and adjectives in sentences and of the suffixes used for forming verbs. As an additional extension activity, they could describe the changes they make to the base words in order to form the verbs. Also ask them to look up the words in an etymological dictionary to find their roots – mainly from Latin and Greek.

100% New Developing Literacy
Word: Structure and Spelling
Ages 10–11
© A & C BLACK

Name the people

- **Look at the words in bold type.**
- **Add the suffix** `er`, `or`, `ian` **or** `ist` **to form a noun for each person from the word in bold.**

I perform **music**.	I look after a **library**.	I **collect** things.	I sell **flowers**.
musician			
I **swim**.	I **translate**.	I **compete**.	I **govern**.
I **lecture**.	I study **biology**.	I do **manicures**.	I **cycle**.
I study **history**.	I **conduct**.	I **supply** goods.	I **style** clothes, hair and so on.

NOW TRY THIS!

- **Write as many words as you can for people who play musical instruments.**

Teachers' note The children will have come across most of the suffixes used on this page but might not have used them with the base words shown here. You could also ask them to describe how a base word changed.

100% New Developing Literacy
Word: Structure and Spelling
Ages 10–11
© A & C BLACK

Singles

- **All these words have single consonants.**
- **Write the missing consonants.**

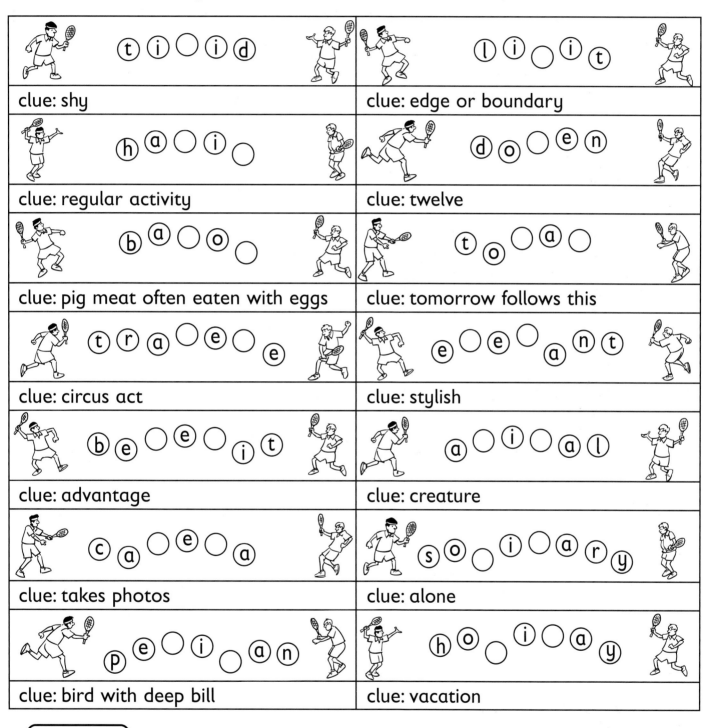

(t)(i)◯(i)(d)	(l)(i)◯(i)(t)
clue: shy	clue: edge or boundary
(h)(a)◯(i)◯	(d)(o)◯(e)(n)
clue: regular activity	clue: twelve
(b)(a)◯(o)◯	(t)(o)◯(a)◯
clue: pig meat often eaten with eggs	clue: tomorrow follows this
(t)(r)(a)◯(e)◯(e)	(e)◯(e)◯(a)(n)(t)
clue: circus act	clue: stylish
(b)(e)◯(e)◯(i)(t)	(a)◯(i)◯(a)(l)
clue: advantage	clue: creature
(c)(a)◯(e)◯(a)	(s)(o)◯(i)(a)(r)(y)
clue: takes photos	clue: alone
(p)(e)◯(i)◯(a)(n)	(h)(o)◯◯(i)(a)(y)
clue: bird with deep bill	clue: vacation

 **NOW TRY THIS!**

- **Write sentences using each word.**

Use a dictionary to check they make sense.

Teachers' note Remind the children of their previous learning about single and double consonants and their effects on the adjacent vowels. If they cannot work out from the clue which letter is missing, ask them to go through the alphabet trying each consonant in turn. For a more challenging activity, you could mask the clues.

100% New Developing Literacy
Word: Structure and Spelling
Ages 10–11
© A & C BLACK

Doubles

- **All these words have double consonants.**
- **Write the missing consonants.**

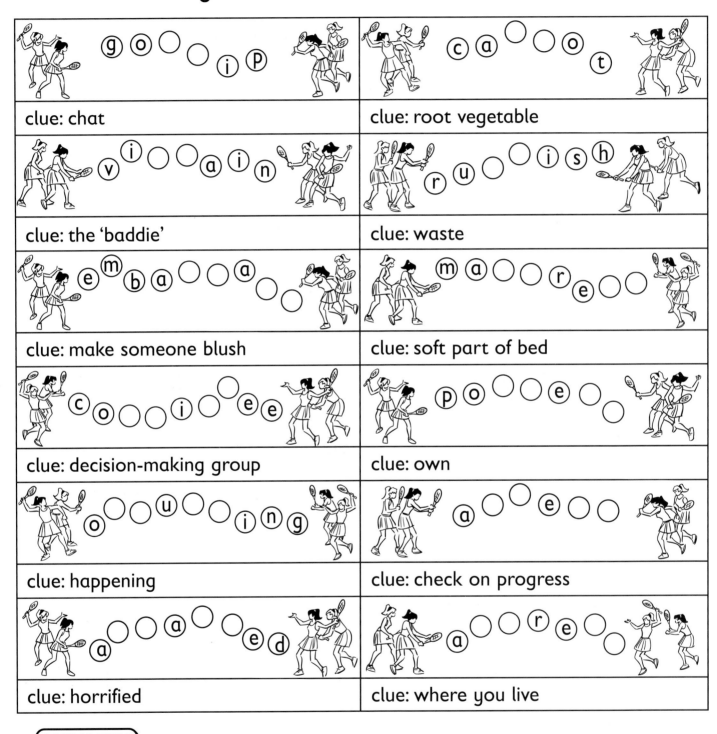

g o ◯ ◯ i p	c a ◯ ◯ o t
clue: chat	clue: root vegetable
v i ◯ ◯ a i n	r u ◯ ◯ i s h
clue: the 'baddie'	clue: waste
e m b a ◯ ◯ a ◯ ◯	m a ◯ ◯ r e ◯ ◯
clue: make someone blush	clue: soft part of bed
c o ◯ ◯ i ◯ e e	p o ◯ ◯ e ◯ ◯
clue: decision-making group	clue: own
o ◯ ◯ u ◯ ◯ i n g	a ◯ ◯ e ◯ ◯
clue: happening	clue: check on progress
a ◯ ◯ a ◯ ◯ ◯ e d	a ◯ ◯ r e ◯ ◯
clue: horrified	clue: where you live

NOW TRY THIS!

- **Write sentences using each word.**

Use a dictionary to check they make sense.

Teachers' note Remind the children of their previous learning about single and double consonants and their effects on the adjacent vowels. If they cannot work out from the clue which letter is missing, ask them to go through the alphabet trying each consonant in turn and checking whether it can be doubled. For a more challenging activity, mask the clues.

100% New Developing Literacy
Word: Structure and Spelling
Ages 10–11
© A & C BLACK

- **All these words have single and double consonants.**
- **Write the missing consonants.**

clue: antonym

clue: very strong wind

clue: a green vegetable

clue: a type of shoe

clue: indoor passage

clue: news programme

clue: precise, exact

clue: not the same

clue: stop breathing

clue: everything you learn at school

clue: not often

clue: behaviour that shows opinions

NOW TRY THIS!

- **Write a sentence for each word.**

Use a dictionary to check the meanings.

Teachers' note Point out that the words on this page contain single as well as double consonants and that in each word the double consonant comes first.

100% New Developing Literacy
Word: Structure and Spelling
Ages 10–11
© A & C BLACK

Mixed doubles

- **Write the answers on the grids.**
- **Write one letter in each box.**

If the answers are all correct the highlighted boxes will spell the plural of a large ape.

> The answers all contain a single and a double consonant.

1 Small antelope.
2 Treacle.
3 The day after today.
4 Popular ice cream flavour.
5 _____ lines never meet.
6 Enormous.
7 Essential.
8 Intimidate.

1		G	A	Z			
2							
3							
4							
5							
6							
7							
8							

- **Circle the correct spellings in each case.**

   1 The millionaire/milionnaire/milionaire has amased/amassed/ammassed her fortune by making shoes.

   2 She remembered a talk given by Proffessor/Professor/Proffesor O'Gready on how to get rich.

   3 She had a dilema/dillemma/dilemma: how to make money while being fair to all the people she dealt with.

   4 To remind herself that she was the same as everyone else she wore a medallion/medalion/meddallion inscribed 'Once you had nothing'.

NOW TRY THIS!

- **Do some research on words that have single and double consonants.**
- **Find out which is the more common: the first or the second consonant being doubled.**

> Focus on nouns and adjectives.

Teachers' note Point out that the words on this page contain single as well as double consonants and that in each word the double consonant comes second. They should check the spellings in a dictionary, including the word running down the highlighted column.

100% New Developing Literacy Word: Structure and Spelling Ages 10–11 © A & C BLACK

Nouns ending **ancy** or **ency**

- **Add the suffix** **ancy** **or** **ency** **to form nouns from other nouns and from adverbs and adjectives.**
- **Rewrite each new sentence using the noun.**

Helen is an **accountant**.	➡ Helen's work is in <u>accountancy</u>.
Mark told us that she is **fluent** in French, German and Arabic.	➡ Mark told us about her _____ in French, German and Arabic.
The office has a **vacant** situation.	➡ There is a _____ in the office.
Helen wondered why staff **frequently** left for other jobs.	➡ Helen wondered about the _____ of staff leaving for other jobs.
She wanted to know how **efficient** the office was.	➡ _____ _____ _____
A clerk had left without being **decent** enough to let the manager know.	➡ _____ _____ _____
People were usually replaced by temporary staff sent by an **agent**.	➡ _____ _____ _____ _____

NOW TRY THIS!

- **Write the base words these nouns come from.**

  tenancy   infancy   delinquency   absorbency

- **Use the words in sentences.**

  Use a dictionary to check the meanings.

Teachers' note Point out that these endings can be added to base words of different classes in order to form nouns. Use sentences to show the different purposes of each type of word. You could also ask the children to collect examples of nouns ending with the suffix **-ancy** or **-ency** (and perhaps also **-ance** and **-ence**) from newspapers.

100% New Developing Literacy
Word: Structure and Spelling
Ages 10–11
© A & C BLACK

25

Noun glossary

- **Complete the glossary of nouns ending with the suffix ☐cy☐ or ☐ty☐.**
- **Describe how the noun is formed.**

Use a dictionary.

Noun	Definition	How to form the noun
anxiety	Being **anxious**.	Remove -ous and add -ety.
	The word for **aristocrats** as a group.	
captaincy	The position of _____.	
	Being **certain**.	
	A society that is run by **democrats**.	
	Being **entire**; the whole of something.	
honesty		
	Being **idiotic**.	
literacy		
naivety		
notoriety		
	Being **numerate**.	
	Being **obstinate**.	
propriety		
	Being **safe**.	
secrecy		
	A **social** group or population.	
truancy		
	Being **urgent**.	
	Being **various**; all kinds.	

Teachers' note Point out that in some parts of the glossary the children should write the missing noun and in others they should write the missing definition, using the existing texts as a clue.

**100% New Developing Literacy
Word: Structure and Spelling
Ages 10–11
© A & C BLACK**

Verb trios

- **Complete the verb trios by adding the suffixes** ed **and** ing .

appalled ← appal → appalling   ← appeal →

← blur →   ← confer →

← console →   ← control →

← dial →   ← fail →

← flare →   ← fuel →

← label →   ← mimic →

← murmur →   ← panic →

← patrol →   ← prefer →

← rival →   ← sponsor →

Teachers' note Remind the children of their previous learning about verb suffixes and about double consonants. They could try writing each missing word on the back of the page to check if it looks right with the final consonant doubled. Note that in many (but not all) verbs ending **l** or **r** the doubled final consonant is in the stressed syllable (see *Notes on the activities*, pages 7–8).

**100% New Developing Literacy
Word: Structure and Spelling
Ages 10–11
© A & C BLACK**

En verbs

- **Rewrite the sentences.**
- **Replace the words in bold type with a verb that begins with the prefix** en .

You might also need to add a suffix.

The new road will **make us able** to get home in 20 minutes.

The new road will <u>enable us to get home in 20 minutes.</u>

The fence **makes the** garden **closed**.

Would you **put me on the roll** for the college, please?

I **put my name on the list** for the course.

I was **in a rage**.

They will **put** children who use them **in danger**.

The extension will **make** the house **larger**.

Teachers' note Point out that the word order will need to be changed when rewriting the sentences but that the meaning remains the same (see *Notes on the activities*, page 8). You could also remind the children of previous learning about similar types of verb, formed from adjectives, with the suffix, rather than the prefix, -en (*lengthen, shorten, widen*).

28

**100% New Developing Literacy
Word: Structure and Spelling
Ages 10–11
© A & C BLACK**

Nationalities

• **Add a suffix to form the nationality.**
**Some country names may
need to change before the
suffix is added.**

Check your
answers in a
dictionary.

Albania	Brazil	Canada
China	Egypt	England
Ethiopia	Finland	France
Iceland	India	Iraq
Israel	Japan	Jordan
Mexico	Morocco	Norway
Poland	Portugal	Russia
Spain	Turkey	Vietnam

Ghana

Ireland

Kenya

Pakistan

Scotland

Wales

**NOW TRY
THIS!**

• **List six other countries
and their nationalities.**

Use an
atlas.

Use a
dictionary.

Teachers' note Use news reports on sports events to introduce nationalities, many of which the
children will know from watching international events such as the Eurovision Song Contest, the
Commonwealth Games and the Olympic Games. Ask them to identify the suffix added to the name
of the country or any other way in which the country's name is altered to form the nationality.

100% New Developing Literacy
Word: Structure and Spelling
Ages 10–11
© A & C BLACK

Material adjectives

- **Look at the words with the suffix** `en` **.They are adjectives that mean made of or like a material.**
- **Write the correct word in each gap.**

Use a dictionary.

Word-bank

| ashen | brazen | earthen | flaxen |
| golden | oaken | wheaten | woollen |

Write whether the adjective means made of or like the material.

Sentence	Meaning of adjective
1 The garden was full of _____ yellow flowers.	
2 A huge _____ table almost filled the room.	
3 She wore _____ socks to keep her feet warm.	
4 Her face was _____ from the shock of seeing the accident.	
5 The huts the poorer Saxons built had _____ floors strewn with rushes.	
6 His _____ hair looked almost white under the strong white spotlight.	
7 The baker specialised in _____ loaves.	
8 There were two tarnished _____ candlesticks on the table.	

- **Look up another meaning of 'brazen' and write a sentence using this meaning.**

NOW TRY THIS!

- **Write the noun each** `en` **adjective is formed from.**
- **Describe how the suffix** `en` **changes the spelling of the base word.**
- **Use a table like this.**

Adjective	Noun formed from	Spelling change

Teachers' note Remind the children how to add the suffix **-en** to adjectives to form verbs: *tighten, loosen*. Show them how it can be added to nouns for materials to form adjectives. Note that some of these mean made of the material (*brazen, earthen, oaken, woollen*) but others can mean either made of or like the material (*ashen, flaxen, golden, wheaten*).

30

**100% New Developing Literacy
Word: Structure and Spelling
Ages 10–11
© A & C BLACK**

Adjective suffixes

- Add the suffix [some] or [ish] to each word to form an adjective.

You might need to change the spelling of the base word by adding or deleting letters.

fear_____	boy_____	fool_____	awe_____	fiend_____
pig_____	bother_____	child_____	burden_____	snob_____
girl_____	ghoul_____	trouble_____	self_____	sheep_____
loathe_____	grey_____	blue_____	owl_____	meddle_____
young_____	quarrel_____	old_____	plump_____	cumber_____
slave_____	slow_____	style_____	fifty_____	white_____

- Write definitions for six adjectives from the table.

Adjective	Definition

NOW TRY THIS!

- **What do you notice about the meanings of most adjectives where [ish] is added to a noun?**
  (Examples: owl, child, fool, fiend)
- **What do you notice about the meanings of most adjectives where [ish] is added to a number?**
  (Examples: thirty, forty, fifty)
- **What do you notice about the meanings of most adjectives where [ish] is added to another adjective?**
  (Examples: grey, blue, white, plump)

Teachers' note Begin by asking the children to identify the nouns and verbs in the table. They could give sentences containing each word to demonstrate its class and meaning. Ask them to compare their answers with those of others in their groups and to use a dictionary to check any discrepancies.

100% New Developing Literacy
Word: Structure and Spelling
Ages 10–11
© A & C BLACK

Spelling poem

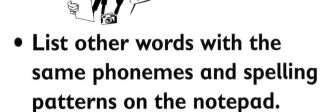

- **Read the poem aloud.**
- **Underline the words with phonemes that can be spelt in different ways.**

- **List other words with the same phonemes and spelling patterns on the notepad.**

Hints on Pronunciation for Foreigners

I take it you already know
Of tough and bough and cough and dough?
Others may stumble, but not you
On hiccough, thorough, laugh and through?
Well done! And now you wish perhaps
To learn of these familiar traps?

Beware of heard, a dreadful word,
That looks like beard and sounds like bird,
And dead: it's said like bed, not bead,
For goodness' sake, don't call it deed!
Watch out for meat and great and threat,
They rhyme with suite and straight and debt.

A moth is not a moth in mother
Nor both in bother, broth in brother,
And here is not a match for there,
Nor dear and fear for bear and pear,
And then there's dose and rose and lose –
Just look them up: and goose and choose,

And cork and work and card and ward
And font and front and word and sword,
And do and go and thwart and cart –
Come, come! I've hardly made a start!
A dreadful language? Man alive,
I'd mastered it when I was five!

Anonymous

tough → rough

 **NOW TRY THIS!**

- **Write your own verse about some other words with graphemes that can stand for different phonemes.**

 Use the poem as a model.

Teachers' note The poem could be read as a whole-class activity, with children taking turns to read a verse. It is likely that they will read words they know wrongly because of their juxtaposition with others that have the same graphemes standing for different phonemes. They could first be given time to read the poem to themselves and to notice this.

100% New Developing Literacy
Word: Structure and Spelling
Ages 10–11
© A & C BLACK

Spelling rhymes

- **Read the poem aloud.**
- **Complete the spelling rhymes table.**

The eminent Professor Hoff
Kept, as a pet, a kangaroo
Who, one March day, started a coff
That very soon turned into floo.

Before the flue carried him off
To hospital (still with his coff)
A messenger came panting through
The door and saw the Kangarough.

The kangaroo lay wanly there
Within the Prof's best armchere
Taking (without the power to chew)
A sip of lemonade or tew.

"O Kangaroo," the fellow said
"I'm glad you're not already daid,
For I have here (pray do not scoff)
Some stuff for your infernal coff.

"If you will take these powdered fleas,
And just a tiny lemon squeas
Mixed with a little plain tapwater,
They'll cure you. Or at least they ater."

Prof Hoff then mixed the medicine,
Putting the fleas and lemon ine
A glass of water, which he'd brought
The Kangaroo as he'd been tought.

The Kangaroo drank down the draught,
Shivered and scowled – then oddly laught
And vaulted out of the armchair
Before the Prof's astonished stair –

Out of the window, in the air
Up to the highest treetop whair
He sat upon the topmost bough
And chortled down, "Look at me nough!"

From *The Kangaroo's Coff* by Anthony Thwaite

Spelling rhymes					
Wrongly spelt word from poem	**Rhymes with**	**Correct spelling of word**	**Wrongly spelt word from poem**	**Rhymes with**	**Correct spelling of word**
coff	Hoff/scoff	cough			

NOW TRY THIS!

- **Write another verse for the poem.**
- **Use words that have different spellings for a rhyming phoneme.**

Use the poem as a model.

Teachers' note The poem could be read as a whole-class activity, with children taking turns to read a verse. Ask them to look for a pattern in the changes in the spellings of repeated words such as *cough*, *'flu*, *kangaroo* and *armchair* as well as the pattern in spelling changes for other words such as *dead, squeeze, in, taught, laughed, stare, where, now.*

**100% New Developing Literacy
Word: Structure and Spelling
Ages 10–11
© A & C BLACK**

Spell that rhyme

- **Write rhyming words in the gaps that are spelt wrongly to match the rhyming graphemes.**
- **Write the correct spellings in the margin.**

Use the word-bank but add other words of your own.

Notice that the rhyme pattern changes after the first verse.

Grandad's Retigherment

Grandad was happy to retire

And spend his time at his leisure.

He said one day, "I'll join a <u>choir</u>

And sing those notes <u>hoir</u> and <u>hoir</u>."

higher _____

_____

_____

_____

_____

One day when singing a holy hymn

He _____

At the door he saw the vicar

_____

_____

_____

Next he wanted to learn to fly

_____

_____

_____

_____

_____

_____

_____

_____

Word-bank

canoe	true
you	clue
brooch	coach
friend	offend
spend	trend
pleasure	treasure
quicker	trick her
sticker	slicker
him	trim
grim	cherubim
sky	eye
sigh	why
plane	train
chow mein	rain
reign	pain
Spain	train
design	shine

_____

_____

_____

_____

_____

_____

NOW TRY THIS!

- **Plan your own poem that uses wrong spellings for rhyming words.**

Teachers' note The children should first have completed page 33 and be aware of the different graphemes that can be used for spelling particular phonemes. A rhyming dictionary will be useful.

100% New Developing Literacy Word: Structure and Spelling Ages 10–11 © A & C BLACK

Read the runes

The Norse invaders and settlers brought this alphabet, made up of signs called runes, to Britain.

Rune	Modern English phoneme	Rune	Modern English phoneme	Rune	Modern English phoneme
ᚠ	f/v	ᛁ	i	ᛚ	l
ᚢ	u	ᛂ	y	ᛜ	ng
ᚦ	th	ᛊ	oo	ᛟ	e (ee before i or a)
ᚩ	o	ᛈ	p	ᛗ	d
ᚱ	r	ᛦ	ks	ᚪ	a
ᚴ	k	ᛋ	s/z	ᚨ	igh
ᚷ	j	ᛏ	t	ᚼ	i/y
ᚹ	w	ᛒ	b	ᛐ	ee
ᚺ	h	ᛖ	e	ᚸ	g
ᚾ	n	ᛗ	m		

• **Write these words using the modern English alphabet.**

Runes	Answer	Runes	Answer
ᛒᚱᛖᛗ	bread	ᛋᚢᛏ	_____
ᚹᚢᚠ	_____	ᚹᛖᚢᚦ	_____
ᚠᚪᛚ	_____	ᚠᛏᚱᛋ	_____
ᚦᚱᚪᛜ	_____	ᚢᚠᚴᚼ	_____
ᛋᛏᛋ	_____	ᚴᛖᛋᚪᛏ	_____
ᛒᚱᚪᛏ	_____	ᚦᚪᛏᛦ	_____
ᚠᚪᛏᛜ	_____	ᛒᚱᛁᛜ	_____
ᛐᛋᛏ	_____	ᚹᛖᛋᛏ	_____
ᚠᚪᛦ	_____	ᚱᛁᛜ	_____

Teachers' note Ask the children to look up each rune in the second word and to say what they think it is. They should consider the phoneme represented by each rune and the different ways of spelling that phoneme using the modern English alphabet.

100% New Developing Literacy
Word: Structure and Spelling
Ages 10–11
© A & C BLACK

Greek spellings

- **This is the Greek alphabet in upper- and lower-case letters.**

Greek letter	Letter name	English phoneme	Greek letter	Letter name	English phoneme	Greek letter	Letter name	English phoneme
Αα	alpha	a, ar (as in *smart*)	Ιι	iota	i (as in *sit*)	Ρρ	rho	r
Ββ	beta	v (as in *very*), sometimes becomes b	Κκ	kappa	k	Σσ	sigma	s
Γγ	gamma	hy (like h then y in *yes*)	Λλ	lamda	l	Ττ	tau	t
Δδ	delta	th (as in *the*), sometimes becomes d	Μμ	mu	m	Υυ	upsilon	ee
Εε	epsilon	e (as in *get*)	Νν	nu	n	Φφ	phi	ph
Ζζ	zeta	z (as in *zoo*)	Ξξ	xi	x	Χχ	chi	ch (as in *school*)
Ηη	eta	ee	Οο	omicron	o (as in *box*)	Ψψ	psi	ps
Θθ	theta	th (as in *think*)	Ππ	pi	p	Ωϖ	omega	or

- **These English words have been written using Greek letters.**
- **Write them using the English alphabet.**

> Omicron has been used for both the long and short ⬚o⬚ phonemes, and iota for long and short ⬚i⬚.

μιδ   _myth_____   ατομ   _____   μονκ   _____

σχολα _____ παντο   _____   φοτο   _____

φον   _____ σκριπτ _____   ατλασ   _____

κριτικ _____ κριπτ   _____   πλαστικ _____

δερμαλ _____ ακροβατ _____   μικροβ _____

κιλο   _____ τελεσκοπ _____   αστρονϖτ _____

επιδεμικ _____ σιμβολ _____   σιλαβλ _____

Teachers' note Ask the children to look up each Greek letter in the first word and to say what they think it is. They should consider the phoneme represented by each Greek letter and the different ways of spelling that phoneme using the modern English alphabet. Tell the children that this alphabet is still used in Greek. Some of them might like to learn and recite it.

100% New Developing Literacy
Word: Structure and Spelling
Ages 10–11
© A & C BLACK

Spell that sign

These signs have been spelt in a way that attracts people's attention.

• Write the incorrectly spelt words correctly.

_____

_____

_____

_____

_____

NOW TRY THIS!

• Collect examples of other signs or headlines with wrong spellings used for fun or to attract attention.

Teachers' note The children could first collect examples of deliberately wrong spellings on signs, advertisements, labels and so on and discuss why they have been spelt in these ways (usually to emphasise rhyme or alliteration, or just to attract attention). They could also explore the Internet use of **ph** instead of **f**: for example, _phishing_.

100% New Developing Literacy
Word: Structure and Spelling
Ages 10–11
© A & C BLACK

Spellchecker poem

This poem has been checked by a spellchecker.

- **Read out a verse for a friend to write.**
- **Compare this with the poem.**
- **Underline the words the spellchecker got wrong.**

I TOLLED YEW SOW

---

1 **Poet Tree with Mist Aches**
I have a spelling chequer.
It came with my pea sea.
It plainly marques four my revue
Miss steaks eye cannot sea.

2
Eye strike a quay and right a word
And weight for it two say
Weather I am wrong oar write:
It shows me strait away.

3
As soon as a mist ache is maid
It nose bee fore to late
And eye can putt the error rite
It's rarely, rarely great.

4
I've run this poem threw it
I'm shore your pleased too no;
It's letter perfect in it's weigh
My chequer tolled me sew.

Sauce unknown

1
_____
_____
_____
_____
_____

2
_____
_____
_____
_____
_____

3
_____
_____
_____
_____

4
_____
_____
_____
_____

NOW TRY THIS!

- **Write sentences using each wrong spelling from the poem correctly.**

Use a dictionary.

Teachers' note The children could work in pairs or you could use this as a dictation activity. If you choose the latter, let them compare their spellings with those in the poem.

100% New Developing Literacy
Word: Structure and Spelling
Ages 10–11
© A & C BLACK

Compound words

- **How many compound words can you find in the directions?**
- **List them on the chart in two sets.**

Start at the car park to the west of the marketplace. Cross the cobblestones to the Old-Time Music Hall and cut through the narrow alleyway (Cowgate) between this and the clock-maker's workshop. This leads to Hilltop Street.

Turn right at the second-hand shop and walk downhill. Take the first right (Wheelwright's Row) and continue past the old draw-well, a row of farm workers' cottages and two large semi-detached houses. The first farm gate on the right opens into a courtyard that has a public footpath sign. Please keep to the right-hand side, away from the cowsheds. Just beyond the farmhouse there is a cattle grid with a gate beside it. Cross this and proceed along the path to the open countryside. Dogs must be on short leads to keep them out of the sheep-pens.

Look out for a stile alongside the hay-meadow. Go over the stile (there is a dog-gate beside it) and turn left, following the drystone wall. At the end of the wall turn left again, walking uphill beside the sawmill. Cross the millstream via the old footbridge and follow the track.

The track follows the river for about four kilometres. Here you will pass two old lime-kilns and the old lead-mine. Do not try to enter the mine. Turn right through the gate just past the mine and follow the old railway line (now a public bridleway – if you cannot find it, ask a passer-by).

When you reach the stationmaster's house take time to look at the platform where the trains came to a standstill forty years ago. It is now a garden centre with a tea-room and shop. You are now halfway along your route. The second half of the route will be published tomorrow.

Compound words			
Without hyphens		**With hyphens**	

NOW TRY THIS!

- **Collect more examples of compound words in other directions for walks.**

Teachers' note By now the children will be able to recognise compound words and to spell them by splitting them into their constituent words. Point out that some compound words have hyphens to avoid ambiguity: what might they buy in *the second-hand shop* (used items) or *the second hand shop* (a part for a clock)?

100% New Developing Literacy
Word: Structure and Spelling
Ages 10–11
© A & C BLACK

Word families from RE

• **Build up word families for these words you might come across in RE lessons.**

Add different suffixes.

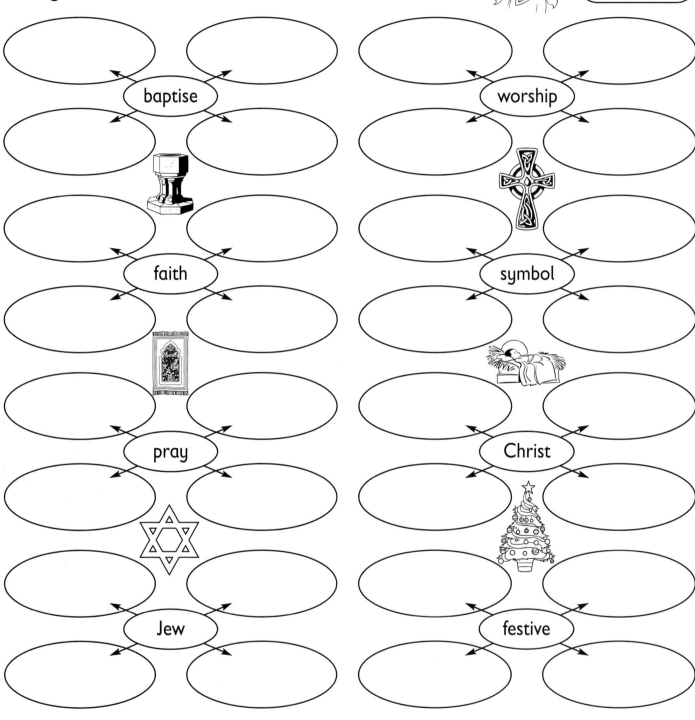

baptise

worship

faith

symbol

pray

Christ

Jew

festive

NOW TRY THIS!

• **Choose two word families.**
• **Write sentences using each word from these.**

Teachers' note Model how to complete the page by filling in the first one with the children: show them how to form different words by adding suffixes to *baptise*.

**100% New Developing Literacy
Word: Structure and Spelling
Ages 10–11**
© A & C BLACK

Word families from science

- **Build up word families for these words you might come across in science lessons.**

Add different suffixes.

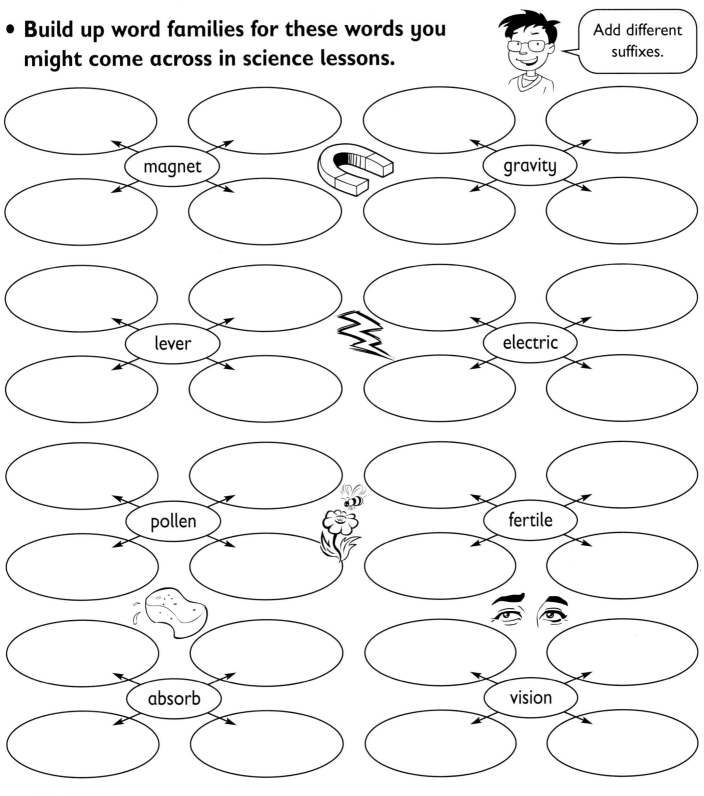

magnet

gravity

lever

electric

pollen

fertile

absorb

vision

NOW TRY THIS!

- **Choose two word families.**
- **Write sentences using each word from these.**

Teachers' note Model how to complete the page by filling in the first one with the children: show them how to form different words by adding suffixes to *magnet*.

100% New Developing Literacy
Word: Structure and Spelling
Ages 10–11
© A & C BLACK

Basic

- **Add or change suffixes to make new words from each base word.**
- **Leave blank any sections you cannot fill.**

You might be able to make more than one noun or verb from some root words.

Make a note of any changes to the root word when you add a suffix.

Base word	Noun 1	Noun 2	Noun 3	Verb 1	Verb 2	Adjective	Adverb	Spelling notes
act	actor	action	activity	act	activate	active	actively	No change to base word
believe								
bury								
collect								
examine								
part								

NOW TRY THIS!

- **Choose two sets of words.**
- **Write sentences using each word from these.**

Teachers' note Discuss the completed example with the children and ask them to use each word in a sentence to demonstrate its meaning. Note that in many cases more than one verb or noun can be formed from a base word.

100% New Developing Literacy
Word: Structure and Spelling
Ages 10–11
© A & C BLACK

42

Back to basics

- Circle the prefixes and suffixes.
- Write the base words.

Some words have more than one prefix and suffix.

(com)press(ion)

press

overreacting

subscription

immigration

undernourished

incalculable

deforestation

incompleteness

enclosure

interchangeable

deregistration

uncontrollable

unsurprising

disconnecting

remorselessness

unconsciousness

NOW TRY THIS!

- Write three other words from each of the base words.

Use a dictionary.

Teachers' note Look at how the first example has been completed to identify the prefix, suffix and base word. Point out that, although *press* is a word found in English, many base words do not appear to be real words because they are from another language, particularly Latin or Greek.

100% New Developing Literacy Word: Structure and Spelling Ages 10–11 © A & C BLACK

43

Peculiar plurals

- **Fill in the missing singulars or plurals of these words from Latin and Greek.**
- **Complete the definitions.**

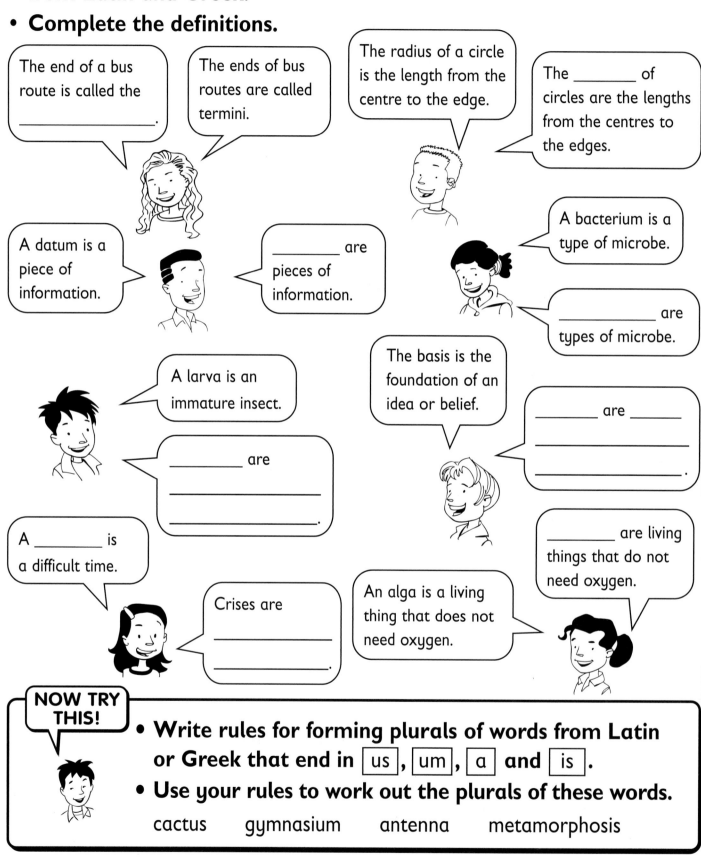

The end of a bus route is called the _____ .

The ends of bus routes are called termini.

The radius of a circle is the length from the centre to the edge.

The _____ of circles are the lengths from the centres to the edges.

A datum is a piece of information.

_____ are pieces of information.

A bacterium is a type of microbe.

_____ are types of microbe.

A larva is an immature insect.

_____ are _____ _____ .

The basis is the foundation of an idea or belief.

_____ are _____
_____
_____ .

A _____ is a difficult time.

Crises are _____ _____ .

An alga is a living thing that does not need oxygen.

_____ are living things that do not need oxygen.

NOW TRY THIS!

- **Write rules for forming plurals of words from Latin or Greek that end in** `us` , `um` , `a` **and** `is` .
- **Use your rules to work out the plurals of these words.**

    cactus   gymnasium   antenna   metamorphosis

Teachers' note Read the first example with the children and ensure that they realise that there is a clue in the second speech bubble. Point out that each example has a similar type of clue. Explain that some Greek- or Latin-based words in English are almost always used in the plural and that many people do not realise this: *data*, *bacteria*, *graffiti*.

100% New Developing Literacy Word: Structure and Spelling Ages 10–11 © A & C BLACK

Be a word archaeologist

- **Find the stories of these words.**
- **Answer the questions.**
- **Write your own questions in any gaps.**

Use an etymological dictionary.

dandelion

What has it to do with lions?

It comes from French *dent-de-lion*, which means lion's tooth.

steward

What has it to do with stew?

_____

_____

somersault

Why isn't it spelt summersalt?

Because _____

_____

February

Why isn't it spelt _____?

Because _____

_____

comb

_____

_____

Because _____

_____

butterfly

_____

_____

bureau

_____

_____

_____

_____

Because _____

_____

Teachers' note Tell the children that this page will explain the unusual or irregular spellings of some English words by helping them to investigate their derivations.

100% New Developing Literacy
Word: Structure and Spelling
Ages 10–11
© A & C BLACK

Homophone sources: 1

Homophones

idle	idol	yoke	yolk	strait
straight	profit	prophet	root	route
beech	beach	tale	tail	chute
shoot	stalk	stork	minor	miner

Definitions

A type of deciduous tree (loses its leaves in winter).	The extension of an animal's backbone.
Someone who predicts events.	Someone who works underground digging out minerals such as coal, tin or diamonds.
The part of a plant that anchors it to the ground and takes in water from the soil.	An image of a god.
The stem of a plant.	A slide, a waterfall.
A harness linking animals such as horses or oxen pulling a cart.	Gain; money gained from trade or business.
Story.	A course or way: for example, to get from one place to another or for the course of a race.
A sandy shore.	The yellow part of an egg.
To fire a shot.	Lesser: the opposite of major; also someone who is not yet an adult.

Teachers' note Use this with page 47. The children should cut out the cards and try to match each word with its definition and derivation. They will need an etymological dictionary or a detailed dictionary such as *The Shorter Oxford Dictionary*. Continued on page 47.

100% New Developing Literacy
Word: Structure and Spelling
Ages 10–11
© A & C BLACK

Homophone sources: 2

Definitions

✂️

A large bird with long legs and a long beak.	A narrow passage of water.
Without a curve or bend.	Lazy, doing nothing, useless, inactive.

Derivations

✂️

Old English *idel* (empty, worthless, lazy).	Old English *bæce* (shore).
Old English *rot* (source, basis).	Old French *profête*, Latin *propheta* (one who predicts).
Old French *minëor, minour* (a person who works in a mine).	Middle English *streght* (stretched).
Old English *geoc* (join).	Old English *sceotan* (send forth, wound or kill with a shot).
Old French *cheoite* (a fall; from *cheoire*, to fall).	Middle English *ydol*, Latin *idolum* (image, form).
Old English *storc* (tall white wading bird).	Old French *rute* (course).
Old English *bece* (beech tree).	Old English *geolca* (yellow).
Old French *estreit* (narrow), Latin *strictus* (drawn tight).	Latin *profectus* (progress, profit).
Old English *tægl* (twisted rope, rope's end), Old Norse *tagl* (tail).	Latin *minorem* (smaller).
Old English *talu*, Old Norse *tala* (talk).	Old English *stela* (stalk, support).

Teachers' note Continued from page 46. Ask the children for some homophones. Why are words with the same sound spelt differently? Discuss how it came about that different things, actions or ideas are known by the same words. Explain that in many cases they came from other languages or from words that were spelt and pronounced differently in Old English, but changed over time.

100% New Developing Literacy
Word: Structure and Spelling
Ages 10–11
© A & C BLACK

Viking invasion

- **Match the Old Norse (Viking language) to the English derivations.**
- **Explain how you think the spelling of the modern word came about.**

breidd	vett, vætt	lagu	broðir*	kambr
knoka	utlagi	kirkja	frecknur	hreindyri

*ð is pronounced like | th | in 'the'.

Modern word	Old Norse word	Spelling explanation
breadth	*breidd*	
brother		
church		
comb		
freckles		
knock		
law		
reindeer		
outlaw		
weight		

NOW TRY THIS!

- **Use Old Norse words to help you to explain the spellings of these.**

  father   height   laugh   sight

  sword   wreck   wrong   yew

Use an etymological dictionary.

Teachers' note Look at the second example with the children and if they cannot identify the corresponding Old Norse word, ask them to move on to the next one. They can return to any they leave blank after they have completed the more accessible ones.

100% New Developing Literacy Word: Structure and Spelling Ages 10–11 © A & C BLACK

Arabic wordsearch

- **Circle the words derived from Arabic that match the definitions.**
- **Write them next to the definitions.**
- **Write them next to the Arabic words you think they come from.**

Check your answers in an etymological dictionary.

C	A	A	Z	A	P	R	I	C	O	T
O	L	M	A	L	L	L	S	L	S	Z
F	C	B	Q	W	W	K	E	B	A	B
F	O	E	F	G	S	J	Q	K	F	L
E	H	R	X	K	H	S	U	G	A	R
E	O	Q	Z	R	E	T	I	G	R	S
A	L	G	E	B	R	A	N	E	I	O
A	X	X	R	N	B	L	X	N	E	F
A	L	C	O	V	E	C	I	I	R	A
F	L	W	M	A	T	T	R	E	S	S

Definitions

1 Drink that can act like a drug. _____
2 A type of mathematics. _____
3 A niche in a wall. _____
4 A yellowish-brown fossil resin used in jewellery. _____
5 A soft fruit with a stone, yellow flesh and a soft yellow/orange skin. _____
6 A hot drink. _____
7 He came from Aladdin's lamp. _____
8 Cooked meat threaded onto a stick. _____
9 Long cushion for sleeping on. _____
10 Nought. _____
11 A cross-country expedition, usually in tough vehicles, such as jeeps. _____
12 A round flat bead sewn onto fabric for decoration. _____
13 Sweet fizzy powder. _____
14 A long padded seat. _____
15 Sweetener. _____
16 Soft white mineral that can be powdered for dusting onto the body after a bath. _____

Arabic words

sukkar _____   jinn _____
kabab _____   sarab _____
safar _____   al-jabr _____
cipher _____   talk _____
al-kubba _____   kahwa _____
suffa _____   anbar _____
matrah _____   albarkuk _____
al-kuhl _____   sikka _____

NOW TRY THIS!

- **Look up the words from the wordsearch and write the meanings of the Arabic words.**
- **Describe how each meaning and spelling was changed when the word became part of the English language.**
- **Describe any patterns you notice.**

Use an etymological dictionary.

Teachers' note The children can begin by circling any words they find in the wordsearch and, as they circle each one, look for the corresponding definition. Once they have completed the word list for the definitions they can try to match each word to an Arabic word. Note that *al* is a definite article in Arabic; several of the words begin with *al* because the article was combined with the word.

**100% New Developing Literacy
Word: Structure and Spelling
Ages 10–11
© A & C BLACK**

Indian inspiration

- **Read how the meaning and spelling of each Indian word changed as it became an English** loan word .
- **Write the English words on the chart.**

Check your answers in a dictionary.

bungalow	curry	dinghy	juggernaut	jungle
khaki	pepper	shampoo	tanker	thug

Indian word	Changes in meaning and spelling	English word
degi	The e became i, n was added before the g and the i became hy. It was a small rowing boat. Now it means an inflatable boat.	
Jagganath	The first a became u and the second er. The ending ath became aut. Jagganath is a Hindu god whose image is carried on an enormous cart in festival processions. Sometimes his followers used to throw themselves under its wheels.	
pippalt	The i changed to e and the alt ending changed to er. Its meaning changed from berry to a type of spice.	
capo	The c became sh, m was added before the p and the o was doubled. It meant massage but now it's a soapy liquid for hair-washing.	
kaki	An h was added after the first k. The meaning changed from dusty to a yellowish-brown material worn by armies in battle.	
bangalo	The first a changed to u and w was added at the end. It meant belonging to Bengal but came to mean a one-storey house.	
jangala	The first a became u, the second was left out and the third became e. Its meaning changed from a dry area to a rainforest.	
thuggee	The gee ending was dropped. It meant a professional robber and murderer. In English it came to mean any rough criminal.	
taku	An n was added before the k and the u became er. It was a large tank for water for crops. In English it is a truck with a large container for liquid.	
kari	The k changed to c, the a to u, the i to y and the r was doubled. It meant any sauce. Now it means a spicy sauce.	

NOW TRY THIS!

- **Write the stories of these loan words.**

  chutney   jodhpurs   pyjamas   tandoori

Use an etymological dictionary.

Teachers' note The children could list any words they know from Indian languages. Discuss how they know them: for example, from foods. Tell them that Indian languages are written with different alphabets. When they are written for people who use the same alphabet as English they are transliterated. This means that there are different ways of spelling them using the English alphabet.

100% New Developing Literacy
Word: Structure and Spelling
Ages 10–11
© A & C BLACK

A Latin root: 1

- **Add prefixes and suffixes to make words to match the definitions.**

The words all have the root ⌐pend⌐ from Latin *pendere* (to hang or to weigh). **If you get all the answers right, the letters in the highlighted column will spell another** ⌐pend⌐ **word.**

Check your answers in a dictionary.

Definitions

1 To hang up.

2 A small thin tube hanging from part of the intestine.

3 Excitement while waiting for something to happen.

4 To rely on or be decided by other events or people.

5 Its old meaning was 'items weighed together'. It now means a collection.

6 Something that hangs. It usually means something (for example, a medallion or charm) worn on a chain around the neck.

7 Its old meaning was 'needing much gold to be weighed out'. Now it means costly.

8 Inflammation of the appendix.

9 Heavy bar that hangs in old clocks and swings to keep time.

10 A place where medicines are prepared and weighed out or measured into packages.

11 About to happen – usually something threatening 'hanging over' a person or people.

- **Write the meaning of the word that reads down the grid.**

NOW TRY THIS!

- **Write nouns formed from the words in** ⌐1⌐ **and** ⌐7⌐ **.**
- **Write a verb formed from the word in** ⌐10⌐ **.**
- **Use these in sentences.**

Use a dictionary.

Teachers' note Use examples such as <u>struct</u>ure, ex<u>tract</u> and <u>audit</u>ion to demonstrate the way in which Latin words have become incorporated into English. Point out the base words that come from Latin and explain that these are sometimes known as roots. The children could work in pairs, reading the clues, with one acting as scribe, writing one letter in each square.

100% New Developing Literacy
Word: Structure and Spelling
Ages 10–11
© A & C BLACK

A Latin root: 2

• **Write the nouns or verbs that match the meanings.**
They all have the segment $\boxed{\text{fact}}$ **or** $\boxed{\text{fect}}$ **,**
from Latin *facere* **(to make or do), with**
a prefix or suffix, or both.

Prefix-bank		Suffix-bank
a	e	ery
arte	in	ion
bene	manu	or
con	per	ory
de		ure

Something which has been done or exists.

fact

A place where things are made.

fact_____

An object that has been made.

_____**fact**

What happens because of something.

_____**fect**

To make a difference to something.

_____**fect**

A fault or flaw.

_____**fect**

Made or done with no faults.

_____**fect**

Someone who does good, especially by giving.

_____**fact_____**

The making of goods.

_____**fact_____**

Cakes and other sweet things that have been made.

_____**fect_____**

To cause an illness or disease by entering someone's body – what a germ does.

_____**fect**

NOW TRY THIS!

• **Form new words by adding other prefixes and suffixes to the words on this page.**

• **Choose six words to write in sentences.**

Useful prefixes and suffixes			
dis	im	ion	ing
ious	ive	satis	

Use a dictionary.

Teachers' note Use examples such as de<u>scend</u>, <u>re</u>duce and col<u>lect</u> to demonstrate the way in which Latin words have become incorporated into English. Point out the base words that come from Latin and explain that these are sometimes known as roots.

100% New Developing Literacy
Word: Structure and Spelling
Ages 10–11
© A & C BLACK

Greek puzzle

- **Use word segments from Greek to form words with the meanings on the jigsaw pieces.**

You might have to change the spellings of the base words.

- **Use a prefix or suffix if necessary.**

Greek base word	Meaning	Greek base word	Meaning		Prefix
aul	pipe	logy	word, speaking		de
bio/be	life	mega	great		**Suffixes**
chrome	colour	metro	measure		ant
geo	earth	micro	small		ate
graph	to write, to draw	mono	alone, single		atry
hydro	water	phone	sound		ed
iatrist	healer	psyche	soul, mind		ic
lith	stone				y

A single standing stone.

A very big stone.

Study (speaking of) the soul or mind.

Mind healer.

A speech by one person.

One colour.

Small sound.

Great sound.

Study (speaking of) life.

For measuring water.

Using water pipes.

A very small living thing.

For measuring small things.

Study (speaking of) the earth.

Writing about or drawing the earth.

With the water taken out.

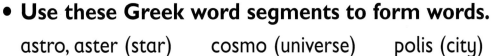

NOW TRY THIS!

- **Use these Greek word segments to form words.**

  astro, aster (star)   cosmo (universe)   polis (city)

- **Write the meaning of each word you have formed.**

Teachers' note Model how to approach this activity through the first example: *I need a word for single … I can see 'single' – 'mono'. Now I need a word for stone: that's it – 'lith'. If I put those two together I can make 'monolith'.*

100% New Developing Literacy
Word: Structure and Spelling
Ages 10–11
© A & C BLACK

Named for the gods

- **Write a word that comes from the name of each Greek or Roman god.**

Check your answers in a dictionary.

Atlas held the Earth on his shoulders.	Ceres was the Roman goddess of crops and seasons.	Echo could only repeat what others said.	Fortuna was the goddess of good luck.
	cer_____		
Hypnos was the Greek god of sleep.	Jove was another name for Jupiter, the main Roman god.	Kronos was the Greek god of time.	The Muses were a group of goddesses who inspired the arts and learning.
	jov_____	chr_____	mus_____
Mnemosyne was the Muse for memory.	Mars was the Roman god of war.	Mors was the Roman god of death.	Vulcan was the Roman god of fire.
	mart_____	mort_____	vol_____

Speech bubbles: "Say that again." "Say that again." "It's ten minutes fast." "I remember leaving my robe at your house 64 years ago." "Die, mortal."

NOW TRY THIS!

- **Write sentences using the words from the chart.**

Teachers' note Remind the children of Greek and Roman myths they have read. Ask them to name some characters, including the gods. Tell them that some names have become English words without being changed, apart from losing the initial capital (for example, *atlas*), but others have been changed slightly. For a more challenging activity, delete the letters provided.

100% New Developing Literacy
Word: Structure and Spelling
Ages 10–11
© A & C BLACK

Word groups

- **Work in a group of five.**
- **Each choose one word from the box.**
- **Take turns to find a word on one of the labels whose meaning is linked to your word.**
- **Explain this to the group.**

grade
note
part
quest
toxin

Cross out each word below after explaining the meaning link.

degrade

request

intoxicate

detoxify

gradual

toxicity

notation

notify

apart

annotate

compartment

toxic

graduate

gradation

questionable

department

apartment

question

notable

inquest

NOW TRY THIS!

- **Write sentences using three other words with meanings linked to each of these.**

  dissolve   dictate   marina   vigil   harmonise

Teachers' note The children should work in groups of five, taking a word each from the list. They make a note of these and then list the others they find that are linked to them. Once these have been found they should be crossed out on this page.

100% New Developing Literacy **Word: Structure and Spelling** Ages 10–11 © A & C BLACK

Vanishing vowels

- **Circle the unstressed vowel phonemes in each word.**
- **Say the word to a friend in a way that helps you to remember how to spell the word.**
- **Write the word to show how you said it.**

ClimATE

clim@te

No thanks, I'll just climb seven.

mackerel

ordinary

literate

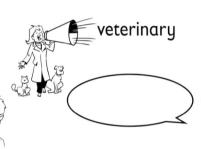

veterinary

extrovert

separate

restaurant

courage

NOW TRY THIS!

- **Split the words on this page into syllables.**
- **In which syllable is each unstressed vowel?**
- **Record your findings in a table.**

Word	No. of syllables	Unstressed vowel syllable
climate	2	2

Teachers' note Ask the children to read the words aloud and to identify the unstressed vowels (there might be more than one in some words). They can then circle these and come up with a 'spellspeak' version of the word to help them to remember them.

100% New Developing Literacy
Word: Structure and Spelling
Ages 10–11
© A & C BLACK

Strange spellings

- **Read the description, then find the word with the strange spelling.**
- **Write the word in the basket.**

This begins normally, with a syllable that rhymes with [sore]. The next letter is silent. The second syllable begins with a hard [g], followed by an unstressed vowel, then a soft [g].

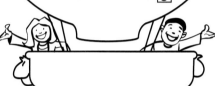

The first two syllables have regular spellings but the third has a vowel phoneme that sounds like [i] but is spelt [ei].

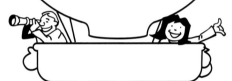

It has two syllables. The first is the prefix [ab]. The second begins with the [s] phoneme spelt [sc] and has a regular [ess] ending.

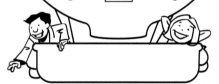

It has three syllables. The first begins with a soft [g] and rhymes with [hen]. The second has one phoneme that sounds like [you]. The last has two phonemes: [i] and [n]. It ends with [e], which makes it look as if the [i] should say [igh].

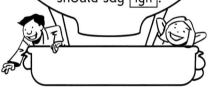

This word, from Italian, has three syllables. The first has two phonemes with regular spellings. The second has two: [s] that sounds like [z], then [a]. The last syllable sounds like [nyuh] but is spelt [gne].

It has five syllables. The first has two phonemes with regular spellings then [s] spelled [sc]. The second has two phonemes. The third has one phoneme and one letter – [a]. The fourth has two phonemes and two letters – [ne]. The last is the suffix [ous].

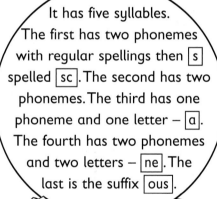

This word has two syllables. The first has two phonemes with regular spellings, but ends with the [k] phoneme spelled [cqu]. The second has one: [er] with a regular spelling.

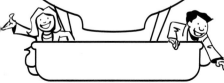

It has two syllables. The first has three phonemes, rhymes with [feet] and has a regular spelling. The second has one phoneme that sounds like [uh] but is spelt [ah].

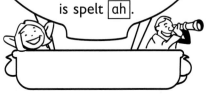

It has two syllables. The first has two phonemes, rhymes with [coo] and has a regular spelling. The second has two phonemes: [k] spelt [qu] then [ai] spelt [et].

Teachers' note Remind the children how to split words into syllables; each syllable contains a vowel phoneme. They should read each description carefully, counting the syllables in the words and looking for the graphemes described. They might find it easier to identify the graphemes and then check that the word fits the description by counting the syllables.

100% New Developing Literacy
Word: Structure and Spelling
Ages 10–11
© A & C BLACK

Help words

- **Read the words.**
- **Circle the tricky part.**
- **Write another word that will help you to spell it.**
- **Tell a friend how this word will help.**

Think about the syllables that are stressed in the help words.

ign(or)ance Help verb _ignore_ _____	victory Help adjective _____ious	resident Help adjective _____
condemn Help noun _____	resign Help noun _____	admiration Help verb _____
environment Help adjective _____	mortal Help noun _____	deference Help verb _____
cooperative Help noun _____	category Help adjective _____	atom Help adjective _____
mechanism Help adjective _____	parent Help adjective _____	palace Help adjective _____

NOW TRY THIS!

- **Choose six pairs of words from this page.**
- **Write sentences using them.**

Use a dictionary.

Teachers' note Show the children how words from the same root as a tricky word can help with its spelling because of changes to phonemes: for example, the **or** in *ignorance* is pronounced 'r because it is an unstressed vowel phoneme, but the same grapheme in *ignore* represents the /or/ phoneme and is pronounced clearly. This helps to act as a reminder of the spelling of *ignorance*.

100% New Developing Literacy
Word: Structure and Spelling
Ages 10–11
© A & C BLACK

Help sentences: 1

- **Complete the sentences to help you to spell tricky words.**
- **Underline the tricky part of the word.**
- **Describe how the sentence helps.**

 There's sand in my <u>sand</u>wich.

 The <u>secretary</u> has a _____.

Peasants eat _____.

_____
_____
_____

_____
_____
_____

_____
_____
_____

His accomplice has _____ in his hair.

 Act your _____ in the passage.

My _____ is on the surface.

_____
_____
_____

_____
_____
_____

_____
_____
_____

 The principal is my _____.

 Pumice stones are often shaped like _____.

Don't _____ for that fallacy.

_____
_____
_____

_____
_____
_____

_____
_____
_____

NOW TRY THIS!

- **Write helpful sentences for spelling these words.**

Each sentence should be connected with the meaning of the word.

| raspberries | canoe | sirloin |

| enclosure | phenomenon |

Teachers' note Point out the first example (*sandwich*) and ask the children what is difficult about spelling this word. Then ask them how the sentence helps. They should notice that *sandwich* has an unspoken **d** but that *sand*, the first part of the word, ends with a spoken **d**. However, the two words come from different roots (see *Notes on the activities*, page 11).

**100% New Developing Literacy
Word: Structure and Spelling
Ages 10–11
© A & C BLACK**

Help sentences: 2

- **Complete the sentences to help you to spell tricky words.**
- **Underline the tricky part of the word.**
- **Describe how the sentence helps.**

That gent is the a<u>gent</u>.

Hang _____ in the palace.

Heather grows on the _____.

_____

_____

_____

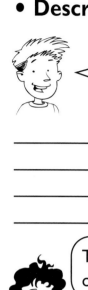
There's a _____ on the tapestry.

The cartoonist drew a caricature of the _____.

You can't keep an orchestra in a _____.

_____

_____

_____

Put the vegetables on the _____.

If you're temperamental you have a _____.

A privilege is not _____.

_____

_____

_____

NOW TRY THIS!

- **Write helpful sentences for spelling these words.**

| raspberries | canoe | sirloin |

| enclosure | phenomenon |

Each sentence should be connected with the meaning of the word.

Teachers' note It helps if the children have first completed page 59. Ask them to read the first example (*agent*) and identify the sentence unstressed vowel. They can then explain how *gent* might help in remembering this unstressed vowel. Ask them to suggest a different sentence to help them to remember it.

100% New Developing Literacy
Word: Structure and Spelling
Ages 10–11
© A & C BLACK

Difficult words

- **Try to read the difficult words in bold type.**
- **Read them aloud with a friend.**
- **See if you can work out their meanings.**
- **Write their meanings.**

Think about …

… the sense of the word in the sentence …

… the class of word: noun, adjective, verb, adverb …

… other word segments you know.

… prefixes you know …

… suffixes you know …

Word in a sentence	Meaning
Those who voted in the election had a choice of three **candidates**.	
Debbie proved what a **polyglot** she is as she answered the questions in many different languages, including Russian, Japanese and Icelandic.	
Dad watched Mark moving around the room talking to people and enjoying their company and said how glad he was that Mark was so **gregarious**.	
He trembled with **trepidation** as he looked at the large audience he was about to address.	
"**Vagrancy** has been made illegal here," said PC Shift as he asked the beggar to move from the shop doorway.	
Ella was in a **quandary**: if she bought the outfit she would not be able to afford to go to the barbecue and if she did not buy it she would have nothing suitable to wear.	
The **sanatorium** was built to provide care for people suffering from tuberculosis.	
"She sings so sweetly," said Gran as she listened to Shazia's **mellifluous** voice.	
The workers complained because the offices were **insufficiently** heated.	

NOW TRY THIS!

- **Choose three of the words above.**
- **Explain how you approached reading them and how you worked out their meanings.**

Teachers' note Read the introduction with the children and emphasise that they can use ideas such as these to help them to read, understand and spell difficult words they come across, using a dictionary only for checking whether they were right.

100% New Developing Literacy
Word: Structure and Spelling
Ages 10–11
© A & C BLACK

Robot words

- **Match each floating word to a word on a robot.**
- **Write it on the robot. Circle the similar letter strings.**
- **Explain to a friend how the word on the robot helps you to read this other word.**

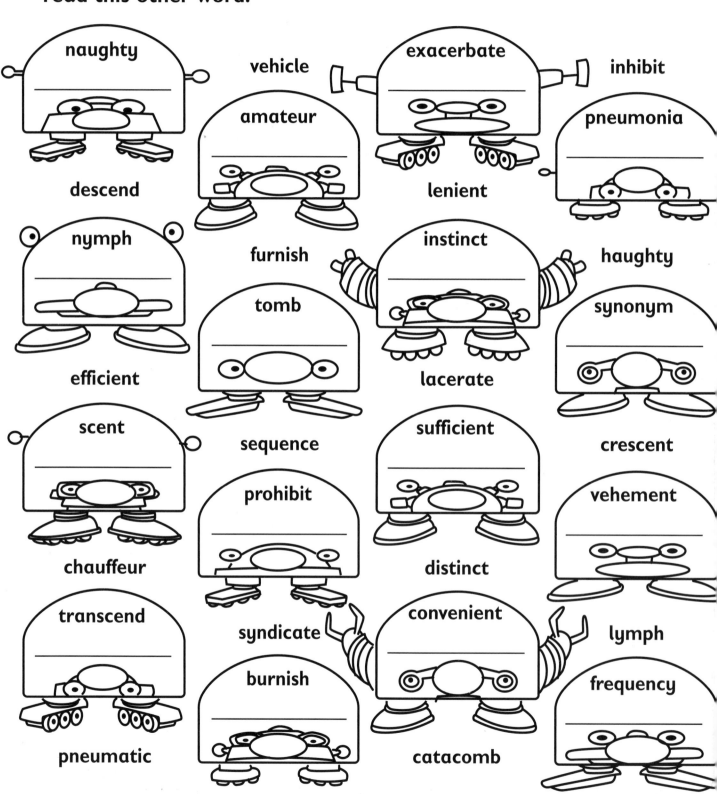

naughty

vehicle

exacerbate

inhibit

amateur

pneumonia

descend

lenient

nymph

furnish

instinct

haughty

tomb

synonym

efficient

lacerate

scent

sequence

sufficient

crescent

prohibit

vehement

chauffeur

distinct

transcend

syndicate

convenient

lymph

burnish

frequency

pneumatic

catacomb

Teachers' note Point out that one way of learning how to spell difficult or irregular words is to think about other words with similar spelling patterns: for example, they will know *naughty* and when they come across *haughty* this will help them to read it.

**100% New Developing Literacy
Word: Structure and Spelling
Ages 10–11
© A & C BLACK**

Acrostics

- **Write an acrostic to help you to remember how to spell each word.**

The sentence should be connected to the word's meaning.

align	seize	siege
All	**S**	**S**
line	e	i
in	i	e
g**reat**	z	g
neatness.	e	e
aghast	**liaise**	**writhe**
A	**L**	**W**
g	i	r
h	a	i
a	i	t
s	s	h
t	e	e
conscience	**appreciate**	**complexion**
C	**A**	**C**
o	p	o
n	p	m
s	r	p
c	e	l
i	c	e
e	i	x
n	a	i
c	t	o
e	e	n

NOW TRY THIS!

- **Practise the acrostics.**
- **Cover the page and write the words.**

Teachers' note Remind the children of the term *acrostic* and explain the structure of an acrostic if necessary. Point out the word *align* and ask the children what is difficult about its spelling. Read the acrostic and ask them how it helps them to remember how to spell *align*. Ensure that they realise that the meaning of the sentence is linked to the meaning of the word. This makes it memorable.

100% New Developing Literacy
Word: Structure and Spelling
Ages 10–11
© A & C BLACK

Flashes of inspiration

- **What makes these words difficult to spell?**
- **Circle the tricky part and write your 'flash of inspiration' to help you to spell the word.**

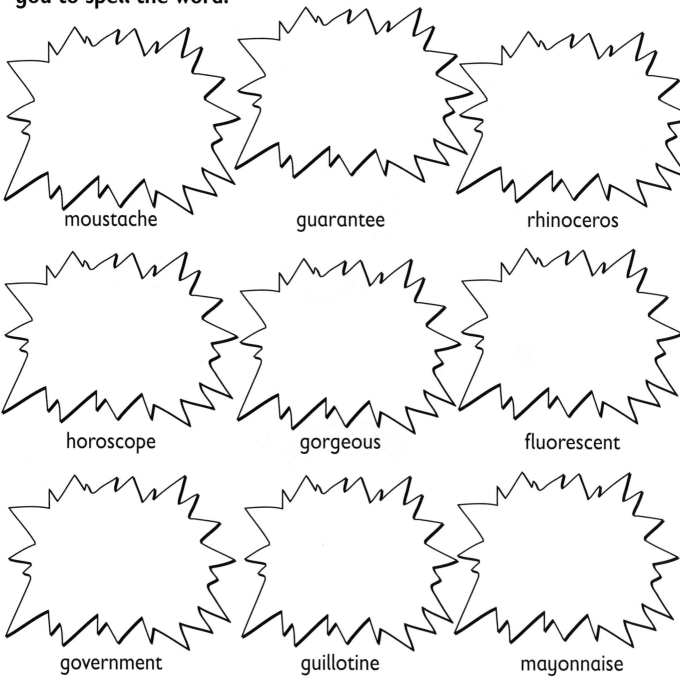

moustache

guarantee

rhinoceros

horoscope

gorgeous

fluorescent

government

guillotine

mayonnaise

NOW TRY THIS!

- **List six other words you find difficult to spell.**
- **Circle the tricky parts and write your flashes of inspiration.**

Teachers' note It is useful if the children have first completed as many activities as possible from pages 55–63. Remind them of the tips provided on those pages for reading, understanding and spelling difficult words. Here their task is to spot the tricky parts of fairly common words and to develop their own strategies for spelling them.

64

100% New Developing Literacy Word: Structure and Spelling Ages 10–11 © A & C BLACK